TRUTH—*Does It Matter?*

An American Atheist Challenges Religious Beliefs

Diane Rogers

TRUTH—DOES IT MATTER?
AN AMERICAN ATHEIST CHALLENGES RELIGIOUS BELIEFS

iUniverse books may be ordered through booksellers or by contacting:

iUniverse
1663 Liberty Drive
Bloomington, IN 47403
www.iuniverse.com
1-800-Authors (1-800-288-4677)

Because of the dynamic nature of the Internet, any web addresses or links contained in this book may have changed since publication and may no longer be valid. The views expressed in this work are solely those of the author and do not necessarily reflect the views of the publisher, and the publisher hereby disclaims any responsibility for them.

Any people depicted in stock imagery provided by Thinkstock are models, and such images are being used for illustrative purposes only. Certain stock imagery © Thinkstock.

ISBN: 978-1-4917-6035-2 (sc)
ISBN: 978-1-4917-6034-5 (e)

Library of Congress Control Number: 2015902508

Print information available on the last page.

iUniverse rev. date: 04/14/2015

Contents

Introduction

I am an atheist. Theism is the belief in a supernatural power, commonly called a god. Atheist simply means not theist, just as atypical means not typical and asymmetrical means not symmetrical. I don't believe in heaven, hell, God, Jesus, Satan, angels, demons, or anything supernatural. I believe in those things that can be proven to exist. Faith is belief without proof.

Of course I can't prove that God doesn't exist, but proving a negative shouldn't be up to me. It's up to the person declaring that God does exist to prove that he does. How about God showing himself in his true form and speaking once and for all to all of us? How come he did just that for people in biblical times? Aren't we even more in need of some sort of acknowledgment from God? Jesus was crucified and declared that he would return. He hasn't been seen or heard from in over 2000 years.

In writing this book, I realized some basic points of agreement must be made between author and reader. We must agree that there is no proof of the more spectacular claims and events told of in the bible other than that they are stated as true in the bible itself.

In order for the bible to contain the infallible word of God, we must believe every statement in it was dictated by God himself to the authors of the bible. No claims made by the bible can be inaccurate because God does not make mistakes. There is no truth to the statement "We must take into account the time in which the bible was written" (actually used as an excuse by the Catholic Encyclopedia), because it was dictated by God and surely he knows the truths that will be revealed in generations to come. Even though the bible says the earth is flat, surely the god who created it knows he created a round earth. Why would he dictate otherwise to his scribes when past, present, and future are known to him?

If human time is not God's time, as apologists suggest when they wish to join creationism with evolution, then all time referenced in the bible should be held to the same standard. Evolution states that the earth is some 14 billion years old and the bible says it is around 6,000 years old. When Moses was on Mount Sinai for 40 of God's days, how many millions of our days was he up there without food or water? How many millions of our days did Noah and his family float on the ark with all those animals? It's ridiculous to say that time as referenced in the bible is not our time. People who say that are just desperately searching for a way to justify their beliefs.

I suspect there are people out there who have serious doubt, but for some reason can't let go of their faith. For them, truth doesn't seem to matter. They believe what they desire to believe, and by wishing make it so. Participating in the rituals is part of their culture.

For most religious people geography, not truth, determines their belief system. People believe what they believe because they live in proximity to other people who believe it. Your parents and all their ancestors believed it. I have a friend who's a devout Catholic. I once told her that if she had been born in Israel to Jewish parents, she would be as convinced that Jesus is not the messiah as she is now that he is. She agreed with me. But that hasn't changed her belief system one bit.

It's sad to see the length to which believers will go in order to justify their faith. One of the major disagreements I have with the religious is that the three major religions (Jewish, Christian, Muslim) depend heavily on revelation. One person, usually a man with no reliable witnesses, says he talked personally with a god. And millions of people just accept his word without question. Moses talked directly with God. How do we know that? The bible says so. How do we know the bible contains truth? We just do. St. Paul talked directly with the heavenly Jesus Christ. How do we know that? The bible says so. How do we know Paul was not hallucinating? The bible says he was not. How do we know the bible contains truth? We just do. Mohammed talked directly with Allah. How do we know that? The Koran says so. How do we know the Koran contains truth? We just do. Joseph Smith was given magical golden plates by an angel named Moroni. How do we know Joseph received those plates when no one but him saw them? He himself told us he did. How do we know Joseph was telling the truth? We just do.

Joseph Smith received no golden plates from an angel. The sacred rock ensconced in the elaborate Dome of the Rock is a piece of a meteor that fell to earth many years ago. Allah did not speak to Mohammed. God in the form of Jesus Christ did not speak to Paul of Tarsus. These men were probably suffering from hallucinations, or simply lying in order to gain attention and fame. Why would God allow a lone man to reveal astonishing truth when he could reveal it to all the people of earth himself? Why are people so eager to believe it? It makes no sense, and has absolutely no evidence to support it.

Please note while reading this book that a great many of the sacred truths of the bible are disclosed by men who had visions.

My references concerning the bible are taken from the King James Version given to me in 1950. My bible says it is "conformable to the edition of 1611 commonly known as the Authorized Version". If your bible does not correspond completely with mine, keep in mind that numerous revisions have been printed over the years.

To me, truth matters immensely. Throughout history mankind has burned with the desire TO KNOW. We should want to know whether or not certain beliefs are true. Scientists have provided us with reliable evidence to support the fact of evolution. The bible provides us with no such evidence to support the fantastic claims of creationism.

Chapter 1

ORIGINS

The bible is a perfect book, written by authors who were inspired by God. Therefore, it has remained unaltered for thousands of years.

The truth is that when this claim is made by the general public it shows their ignorance of bible history, and when it's made by clergymen it shows their intent to deceive the faithful. The truth is that both the old and new testaments have undergone debate and change for more than two thousand years. The protestant church did not agree on which books were inspired by God until 1647, at the Assembly of Westminster.

The truth is that the old testament is nothing more than a collection of scraps written by unknown authors at an unknown time.

The truth is that Moses was not the author of any part of the old testament. In fact, I do not believe Moses was a real person at all. Just like in the case of Jesus, there is no evidence outside the bible itself that says he ever existed, even though he is such a formidable presence in the old testament. He defied the mighty pharaoh and valiantly led his people out of Egypt. He served as an intermediary between God and the chosen people. He dragged the entire Jewish population through the desert for 40 years. (The distance from Egypt through the Sinai is a mere 400 kilometers.) Intense research by scientists and religious zealots alike have not uncovered any historical evidence of Moses. Christian archeologists have never found any evidence of a Hebrew presence in the Sinai desert, even though they supposedly wandered around for 40 years in said desert. Although there are many artifacts and much written evidence proving the existence of many of Moses' contemporaries, there is not one single mention of Moses. There exists no evidence that the exodus ever occurred. The same holds true for the plagues of Egypt and the enslavement of the Jews. This in spite of the fact that at that time Egypt had an advanced and highly literate culture.

No one knows who wrote the old testament. In ancient Iron Age days, a tribe of nomads who were roaming the desert area of the middle east invented their own god to explain natural events that at the time were inexplicable. They had no contact with other nations, no written language, and were illiterate. They never intended their god to be the god of any other tribe or culture, about which they knew nothing. For two thousand years their beliefs were nothing more than oral stories. Eventually some of the stories were written down by various unknown men. Since there were many unknown authors writing randomly, the stories were never compiled into one book. In other words, there is not one original and complete text of the entire old testament in existence. Furthermore, there is not one original and complete text of even one book of it. The old testament is made up of nothing more than written fragments of oral stories told by a variety of nameless men somewhere between 1000 and 50 BCE. Eventually rabbis began piecing the fragments together to form one volume. The Jews were at that time quite comfortable with editing and reediting. This practice was well known and accepted.

The first attempt to finalize the old testament was probably around AD 90 at the Council of Jamnia, or as many scholars believe, the Synod of Laodicea which met in 365. In other words, the exact date at which the books of the old testament were agreed upon is unknown.

Lost books of the old testament were never recovered, and the old testament is only a part of Hebrew scripture that once existed.

"The Jews, having been at some times careless, and at other times profane, they suffered some of the sacred books to be lost through their carelessness, and have burnt and destroyed others." (St. Chrysostom)

The finalized Jewish canon contains 39 books. Protestants recognize the same 39 books as comprising the old testament. Roman Catholics at the Council of Florence in 1442 recognized 7 additional books as canon in their Old Testament, making the total 46.

Why the discrepancy in the old testament? In 1534, Martin Luther translated the Catholic bible into German. He grouped Tobit, Judith, 1 and 2 Maccabees, Wisdom of Solomon, Ecclesiasticus, and Baruch at the end of the bible and declared them Apocrypha (books not to be called sacred canon, but worthy to be read for enlightenment) He is assumed to have done this because to his mind God had first made himself known to the Hebrews, so they should know which books should be included in the canon of the old testament. Therefore the correct canon should be the original 39 books.

Ancient biblical scrolls were found in 1947 in a cave in Qumron, located on the Northwest shore of the Dead Sea. Ten years later eleven caves located in the same area were found to contain tens of thousands of scroll fragments dating from the third century B.C. to A.D 68. These Dead Sea Scrolls are 1000 years older than the fragments used to make up the old testament. In 1956, a man named Father Roland de Vaux was appointed by the Vatican to maintain strict control over the scrolls. Strangely (or not so strangely), some of the scrolls disappeared. Even though the scrolls were of Jewish origin, no Jews were permitted to examine them. A furor began and suspicions arose concerning the Vatican's secrecy and slow progress toward publication. The suspicion was that the Roman Catholic Church was refusing access to the scrolls to those who could not be trusted to promote the dogma of the Catholic faith.

In 1991 unauthorized photos of the unreleased scrolls were published by the Biblical Archaeological Society, and the scrolls became available to scholars. Now more than 50 years later, no one knows the entire truth about the scrolls. Were some destroyed? Most are simply fragments. Of course there is absolutely no reason to assume, if you are a believer, that the majority of these scrolls which predate the old testament are not sacred. How could any believer possibly know that the newly discovered scrolls of antiquity were not inspired? And who knows? Perhaps more ancient scrolls will be found in the future. In order to offset rogue future findings, Catholics and Protestants have closed their canons. "But in regard to the canon itself, which they so superciliously intrude upon us, ancient writers are not agreed. Let the mediators, then, enjoy their own as they please, provided we are at liberty to repudiate those which all men of sense, at least when informed on the subject, will perceive to be not of divine origin." John Calvin

It seems that the book of Esther, included in the official canon, has become controversial and somewhat of an embarrassment.

To emphasize the disagreement over what should and should not be canon in the bible, we have Martin Luther saying "I so hate Esther and II Maccabees that I wish they did not exist. There is too much Judaism in them and not a little heathenism."

As regards the canonized book of Ruth, Thomas Paine stated in his Age of Reason: "Having now shown that every book in the bible from Genesis to Judges is without authenticity, I come to the book of Ruth, an idle bungling story foolishly told, nobody knows by whom, about a strolling country girl creeping slyly to bed with her cousin, Boaz. Pretty stuff indeed to be called the word of God!" (Girls just cannot get a break when it comes to the bible)

Why does all this matter? It matters because believers imagine that the old testament is the official word of God and came about in a simple way - from God's mouth to Moses' ear. But debate over the ancient fragments and what should and should not be included in the bible has raged for centuries. Which of the many authors were actually inspired? How do we know those excluded were not inspired? Why didn't God communicate directly as to the books that comprised his message?

If you believe Moses was in fact a real person, it is nevertheless known that he could not have been the author of the old testament. The great majority of knowledgeable theologians agree, even though they choose not to enlighten the faithful. The old testament contains details of the death and burial of Moses. Would he have written of his own death? Money was not yet invented in the biblical lifetime of Moses, but is written of in the old testament. Many towns are mentioned that were not in existence at the time of Moses. If Moses did write the old testament, why is it filled with laws that are not appropriate for desert nomads?

If the old testament is the word of God, surely he was revealing truths original to himself alone, but it's evident that the unknown authors were only copying earlier texts.

"Tear down your house, I say, and build a boat. These are the measurements of the boat as you shall build her: let her beam equal her length, let her deck be roofed over like the vault that covers the abyss; then take up into the boat the seed of all living creatures" (The Epic of Gilgamesh, 2500 BC)

Moses was turned out to sea in a basket of rushes. This tale originated in the middle east about a thousand years before the story in Exodus. The original river was the Euphrates, and the goddess Ishtar saved an infant king by setting him adrift.

God gave Moses tablets of stone containing his ten commandments. But before that, the god Shamash gave stone tablets containing remarkably similar commandments to Hammurabi.

In Genesis, God tested Abraham by ordering him to kill his son Issac and present him as a burnt offering. But God relented and allowed him to sacrifice a ram instead. In an earlier tale, Agamemnon was about to sacrifice his daughter when the goddess Diana substituted a goat at the last minute.

There are many religious stories older than the ones in the old testament. The Persian god created the world in six days and then he rested. The

Persians, Greeks, Egyptians, Chinese and Hindus had dogma identical to the Garden of Eden and the Tree of Life. They likewise had the story of the fall of man and the serpent. The Chinese said that sin came into the world by the disobedience of women. And even the Tahitians said that man was created from the earth and woman from one of his bones. A great number of old testament tales have their origins in pagan mythology. Almost all ancient religions included a flood myth.

Some believers in the literal truth of the bible have even suggested that Satan himself planted evolutionary evidence such as dinosaur bones, fossils, and carbon dating in order to lead us away from God's true story as told in Genesis. They also suggest the earlier myths that the bible mimics were planted by Satan in order to make us doubt the originality of God's word. Either God has no control over the actions of Satan, or God and Satan are engaging in deliberate acts of deception. If believers accept these theories, there is nothing they won't believe and it's useless to attempt rational discussion with them. Apparently God and Satan are having a good laugh at our expense, playing games and deliberately hiding evidence so that we may have "faith".

If the bible is God's word and is to be believed, why are there so many versions of it? The King James, the New International Bible, the Revised Standard Version, The Living Bible, The World English Bible, and the New King James are but some of them. And revisions are going on right now. I find it interesting that some of these revisions are intended to make the bible more gender friendly. These tactics show that religion is simply fantasy created by mortals who are terrified of death. If people didn't have to die, there would be no need for religion. We are told in Revelation that we are to believe every word of both the old and the new testaments and not alter or add to the originals on pain of exclusion from God's kingdom.

The word "canon" as it relates to the bible is defined as an officially accepted list of books. You may glean from that that there were many books discovered, but not all were accepted. Discussion and argument has gone on for centuries concerning what should be included and what should be omitted. It would be beneficial if we could hear from God just which books he inspired and which he did not.

Many believers claim that while the old testament may not be based entirely on fact, the new testament is a much more reliable source for Christians.

"It is reported in the supplement of the Council of Nicea that the Fathers, being very perplexed to know which were the cryphal (true) or apocryphal (doubtful) books of the old and new testaments, put them pellmell on an altar and the books to be rejected fell to the ground. It is a pity that this elegant procedure has not survived." (Voltaire (1694 – 1778)

Martin Luther was known to dislike the book of Revelation. He remarked that it closely resembled the dreams of the mad abbot Joachim, known to suffer from wild hallucinations about the end of the world. Many reputable biblical scholars regard Revelation as fiction.

We have been led to assume that the gospels according to Matthew, Mark, Luke, and John were inspired along with the writings of Paul. And indeed the only source we have for eyewitness accounts of Jesus are found in those four New Testament gospels. But were these men actual associates of the earthly Jesus, or were they merely recording hearsay? The four authors of the gospels never said they had personally witnessed the miracles of Jesus. In fact, the gospels were written many years after the death of Jesus. Luke 1: 1-2 and Matt 28:16 both say that their accounts concerning Jesus and his miracles were simply passed down to them from earlier generations. Many biblical scholars date the gospels as late as 70-90 C.E., since early Christian writers did not mention them before that time. Had they known of the gospels, they most certainly would have relied upon them to bolster the faith.

But there is one more very good reason to disbelieve the new testament. Once the rational among us accept the fact of evolution, there remains no more truth to the story in Genesis. If Adam and Eve are fictional characters or a metaphoric reference, there was no original sin. When original sin is done away with, there is no need for a god to murder his son in order to satisfy his lust for blood sacrifice to atone for said sin. One cannot accept evolution and still be a Christian because evolution destroys with finality the very reason Jesus' life was made necessary. Even if you reject evolution, wasn't it enough for Adam and Eve to be ejected from the garden for eating a piece of fruit? Do all of us, especially the females, have to grovel and apologize for all eternity?

At least the new testament is original.

The truth is that almost all the religions of the world, including Christianity, have their origins in the worship of the sun. Their gods are born without sexual intercourse on or around December 25th.

The Greeks and Romans had many stories with a god impregnating a mortal woman who was also a virgin. In every case, she bore a child. In most cases, the child was male. He usually had super human skills and eventually became a god himself.

Mithra was a god who predated Jesus. He was called the good shepherd, the redeemer, the savior, and the messiah. Mithraism was the most popular religion in the Roman empire, and was introduced about two generations before the birth of Jesus. Because the dogmas of Mithraism and Orphism are so very similar to Christianity, it's impossible that the similarities are coincidental.

Mithra was the son of a god. Mithraists used bells, candles, and holy water when conducting their services. The details of the last supper of Jesus correspond identically to the last supper of Mithra-right down to the twelve followers present with him and the eating of the body and drinking of the blood. God-eating was common in many ancient religions.

Orpheus was the son of the god Apollo. Orphism taught that the human soul lived on after death – either in eternal torment or eternal bliss. Orpheus was miraculously born and likewise resurrected after his death. Rituals included a holy meal of bread and wine which changed into the body and blood of Orpheus when eaten.

The god Orion walked on water, died, was resurrected, and rose to heaven to take his place as a god.

The Greek god Dionysus was the son of Zeus. He also rose from the dead.

Three thousand years before Jesus rose from the dead, Osiris rose from the dead. And thousands of years before Osiris, the pagan goddess Eastra rose from the dead. Rabbits and eggs were commonly used as sacrifices to her.

There is no recorded historical evidence to prove that Jesus Christ ever existed. (The bible is not recorded history) This in spite of the fact that many historians lived in the same locale and at the same time as the supposed son of God. The bible portrays Jesus as being wildly famous as a prophet and healer. If we are to believe biblical accounts; high priests, Roman authorities, and both rich and poor among the common people knew him and followed him. But not one person who was alive during Jesus' lifetime wrote a single word about him.

In Luke 23:44-45 we learn that there was a three hour eclipse that no astronomer anywhere in the world recorded. And there were astronomers and historians working at that time and in that vicinity. Pliny the Elder and Seneca were two of the better known, but there were others such as Ptolemy, Tacitus, and Suetonius. They recorded other eclipses but not this one.

How about the earthquake mentioned in Matthew 27:51-54 where the earth shook violently, rocks ripped apart, and graves opened permitting saints to rise up and walk around Jerusalem? Local historians failed to mention that also. The bible even says that many people were eyewitness to this remarkable event. Graves opening and zombies walking about in plain view were not happenings unusual enough to mention?

In Matthew 2 Herod was so worried about the baby Jesus that he had all the children in Bethlehem murdered. Wouldn't you think historians would have written of such an atrocity? Not a word even though the area in and around Jerusalem was a lively center of education and record keeping.

The bible also mentions many scribes who were followers of Jesus. But we have zero accounts from any of his contemporaries. Philo Judaeus was the greatest Jewish philosopher and historian of his time. (20 B.C.E to 50 C.E. - the same time as Jesus) He wrote in detail of all events occurring in Jerusalem and the surrounding area. In all his many writings, we find nothing about Jesus.

Matthew 4:25 says that great multitudes of people followed Jesus about in order to hear his message. Luke 12:1 even says that people were literally walking over one another just to get a glimpse of him. Luke goes on to say in 5:15 that huge crowds gathered wherever he went. If such was his fame that people were stampeding over one another to see him, why didn't even one person write an account of any of this?

Following is a list of very prominent historians, poets, and philosophers who were contemporaries of Jesus' and wrote of events occurring during his supposed lifetime. None mention Jesus or the spectacular events the bible ascribes to his life and crucifixion : Seneca (4BCE – 65CE) was Rome's most prominent writer who tracked natural events such as earthquakes and eclipses. Pliny the Elder (23-79CE) wrote 37 books on natural events such as earthquakes, eclipses, and claims of healers. Plutarch (46-119CE) traveled extensively from Rome to Alexandria and wrote of the happenings there. Justus was a first century Jewish writer who lived in Galilee during the era of Jesus.

Apologists love to mention Jewish historian Josephus (37-100 CE) who (supposedly) claimed in his Antiquities of the Jews : "Now there was about this time Jesus, a wise man, if it be lawful to call him a man, for he was a doer of wonderful works, a teacher of such men as receive the truth with pleasure. He drew over to him both many of the Jews and many of the Gentiles. And when Pilate, at the suggestion of the principal men amongst us, had condemned him to the cross, those that loved him at the first did not forsake him, for he appeared to them alive again the third day as the divine prophets had foretold. These and ten thousand other wonderful things concerning him and the tribe of Christians so named from him are not extinct at this day."

While Josephus was a highly respected Jewish historian, his paragraph concerning the Christ has no validity. It is considered by most religious scholars to be a testimony inserted into his account by much later Christian forgers. If Josephus himself had written it, church fathers in the following 200 years would definitely have mentioned it. Not a single person quoted from the Testimonium Flavionum until over 200 years after the death of Josephus. It is known that Christian historians read his works extensively, but not once did they refer to the Jesus account- the very thing that would have strengthened their position. Josephus was not a contemporary of Christ. The birth of Jesus has been ascertained by biblical scholars to be around 5 BC, and his death around AD 33. Josephus lived from 37-100 CE. Even if you persist in believing it was written by Josephus, this testimony is nothing but hearsay. When did hearsay become a reliable method of proof? Josephus was a very well known and prolific Jewish historian who wrote of Jewish history. In all of his other extensive writings, there is no reference to anything remotely resembling the fantastic claims of Christianity. But Christians cling desperately to this one short paragraph among hundreds of pages. Origen, a devout church father of the third century quoted extensively from Josephus, but never mentioned this paragraph. Why? Because it was not added to Josephus' writings until two hundred years after his death. Finally, the paragraph right before the Jesus testimony deals with protests accusing Pilate of attacking the Jews. Immediately following, we have the Jesus paragraph. The very next paragraph begins with "And another terrible misfortune confounded the Jews." The Jesus account is awkwardly wedged between two paragraphs which would flow perfectly without the testimonium.

Read the words of highly regarded leaders of the faith such as Eusebius, acknowledged as the Father of Church History. He stated in his Preparation of the Gospel: "It will be necessary sometimes to use falsehood as a remedy for the benefit of those who require such treatment." Another writing of his was entitled, "How it may be Lawful and Fitting to use Falsehood as a Medicine, and for the Benefit of Those who Want to be Deceived"

In the words of Cardinal Newman: "The Greek fathers thought that when there was a just cause, an untruth need not be a lie. As to the just cause, the fathers make them such as these: self-defense, charity, zeal for God's honor, and the like."

The venerable St Jerome: "There is nothing so easy as by sheer volubility to deceive a common crowd or an uneducated congregation."

If there is no record from any of his contemporaries proving that Jesus was an actual figure in history, why do so many people believe he did in fact live? Even people who deny his divinity believe he was a real historical figure. Since so many people have always believed it, it just wasn't thought of to question his existence. In the same way, people never questioned the belief that the earth was flat until it was proven not to be.

What we know about Jesus comes only from hearsay. We now know that the first of the gospels came into existence some forty years AFTER the death of Jesus. The authors of the four gospels were not contemporaries of Jesus. While the majority of biblical historians today accept that the gospels were not written by the men traditionally named as the authors, many save face by claiming that the Gospels are still based on factual evidence passed down orally. Again, hearsay. There's a very good reason it's not accepted in court.

Chapter 2

ATROCITIES, OBSCENITIES, AND SILLINESS

God's nature is that of a loving and compassionate father. The bible is so beautifully written that it is impossible it was wholly created by mortal men. It must have been inspired by a loving God.

Truth: People who say this have never actually read the bible, and are familiar only with the passages clergy chooses to read to them. But the bible contains many bloodthirsty and unnecessarily cruel passages, making it incongruous with a merciful and loving God. Many of the sacred passages are just plain silly!

Read 2CHR 13:16-18 and find that God favors the children of Judah over the children of Israel and allows the former to slay five hundred thousand Israelites.

The men of Beth-she-mesh dared to look into the sacred ark and for this indiscretion God "smote" more than fifty thousand of them. Read it in 1 Sam 6:19.

In Numbers 16: 32-33 a man named Korah questions Moses' leadership. God becomes incensed and causes a large hole to appear in the earth so that he can swallow up all of Korah's family- men, women, and children- but not before he warns Moses and Aaron to save themselves by running away. In Numbers 16:45-49, God kills two hundred fifty men who irritated him by burning incense.

Many passages are found in the book of Joshua describing his battles. The book of Joshua tells of the battle of Jericho which was so revered that it was immortalized in song. God allows Joshua's army to run amok in Jericho. They are to kill the entire population. Young, old, male and female are to be slaughtered. They are also ordered to slay all the oxen, sheep, and donkeys. From Jericho, Joshua's army marches to Ai and God tells Joshua to do the same in Ai as he did in Jericho. (Joshua 8:2) The citizens of Ai attempt to escape Joshua's army, so God assists Joshua by making the sun and the moon stand still so that there will be more light to kill more people. The ancients thought the sun and moon moved, but shouldn't God know better? God decides even more people need to die, and so he aids Joshua by throwing boulders from heaven down upon the retreating army of Ai. The book of Joshua contains many more horrid descriptions of carnage, all of which are sanctioned by God. There are no exceptions for women, the aged, or children. That is one bloodthirsty deity.

In Joshua, God helps the Israelites slay their enemies; but as we have seen, they don't always escape his wrath. Read the following bible verses depicting horrendous acts of infanticide perpetrated by God: He turns the chosen people into cannibals in Lev 26:29 and Jer 19:9, ordering them to eat their own children. In Ezekial 20:26, the supreme deity heinously orders a burnt offering of all newborns. Why? Because the people are not obeying his laws.

Read Hosea 13:16 wherein God is fuming because the people of Samaria have displeased him. He therefore causes the men to be slain, their children chopped into pieces, and their pregnant wives ripped open.

God threatens to cause wild animals to carry children away in Lev. 26:22

These are by no means the full extent of the maniacal antics of God. One cannot help but think that the authors of the bible delighted in fabricating horror stories in order to frighten followers into submission.

But enough blood and gore for now. We need some comic relief:

The book of Isaiah says that God wanted Isaiah to walk around Egypt naked and barefoot for three years as a wonder for the Egyptians. I guess they would indeed wonder. They wondered why God wanted Isaiah to walk around naked. And for three years?

The daughters of Lot decide to get their father drunk so that they can have sex with him. (Gen 19:31-35)

God and Adam search among the animals of the earth for a "partner" for Adam. This seems creepy.

The story of Solomon's temple is a bit shaky. (1 Kings 5:13-16) (1 Kings 6:2) It was supposedly ninety feet long, 30 ft wide, and 45 ft high. For such a small building, it took a lot of men and years to construct. (183,300 men and 7 years) The bible says the temple contained 9,200,000 pounds of gold and 92,000,000 pounds of silver. (1 Chron 22:14) It seems strange that archeologists have never found even a small piece of it.

At the moment Jesus breathed his last, apparently men rose from their graves and wandered around Jerusalem. These were supposedly saints who had fallen asleep. Did they eventually return to their former lives, or did they go back to their graves? And why didn't any of the contemporary historians who lived in the area write about the marauding zombies? (Mat 27:50-53)

The devil finds God one day and the all-knowing God asks him where he has been lately. (Apparently God doesn't know) The devil says he has been walking around earth observing the wickedness of the people. God boasts that Job is a godly man who is essentially perfect. Satan disagrees and says that Job would curse the name of God if all his possessions were taken away. Since boredom is such a problem for supernaturals, the two embark upon an amusing way to settle the dispute. God gives Satan permission to do anything he wants to Job as long as he does not kill him. In the familiar story, Satan afflicts Job with disease, slaughters his livestock, murders his family, and kills his workers. Job remains faithful to God even in the face of all this adversity. The absurdity of this tale lies in the supposed fact that God is all powerful. Why does he need to prove his point to Satan? Why would he allow Satan to murder so many innocents? Is it just a way to pass the time? Read the story in Job 1:1-12.

Does anyone seriously believe that Sarah was one hundred years old when she gave birth, and Abraham was well past one hundred when he became a father? Abe was not the oldest biblical father, however. Noah was five hundred years old when he had three sons. (Genesis 18:11-15, 21:1-2, and 25:1-2.

One of the many things that should lead you to doubt the beauty of the bible is that God has an absurd preoccupation with sex, virginity, and genitals. It doesn't seem like a quality to be admired. God states in Deuteronomy 23:1-2 that any man who is injured in his genitals may not attend worship. If a man is born out of wedlock, he may not attend worship unless he knows the names of his ancestors to ten generations. It seems doubtful that anyone living at that time would know his ancestry that far back. It is probable that most people living right now do not. But the bigger question is: Why does God care about genitals so much? And how would the local priest know the condition of a man's genitals? Are they examined at the door before admittance? There are passages too numerous to count containing ridiculous rules, regulations, and punishments relating to sex and virginity. They will be discussed in detail in later chapters. (Think oppression of women)

God is obsessed with bodily functions in passages such as Isaiah 36:12, II Kings 18:27, Ezekial 4:12, I Kings 14:10, and Malachi 2:3. What do these five passages have in common? They all contain references to "piss and dung". It seems that God has a great compulsion to spread the aforementioned onto the faces of those who displease him. In some cases, he orders the offenders to eat the same.

Read Song of Solomon, which some claim to be beautiful poetry. God isn't mentioned anywhere in the Song of Solomon. This book tediously lists all the body parts of the beloved in simile. The beloved's thighs are like jewels, navel like a goblet, belly like wheat surrounded by lilies, breasts like roes that are twins, and teeth like a flock of sheep. The lover laments that the beloved is not akin to someone who sucked on his mother's breasts.

A physical description of God occurs in Psalms 18:8. Flames shoot from the mouth of God, and smoke spews from his nostrils. That's right. God's mouth is on fire and his nostrils are smoking. It's probably because in places like Jeremiah 25:30 we learn that God needs a mouth to roar and shout. Read Genesis 8:21 and you will learn that God loves the scent of burning animals. He even wants us to sacrifice the fat from animals to him. (Leviticus 3:16)

The old testament contains a large number of rules concerning animals. This seems odd because there are so many more important things to worry about. (Murder? War? Starvation? Poverty? Disease? Etc. etc.) God is very adamant in forbidding certain practices. We may not boil a kid (young goat) in its mother's milk. (Deuteronomy 14:21). We may not plow a field with an ox and a donkey on the same yoke. (Deuteronomy 22:10) We may eat anything that has fins and scales, but not shellfish. (Lev. 11:3 and Deut. 14:6) We may eat any animal that has "cloven hooves and chews its cud", but other land mammals are forbidden. (Lev. 11:3)

One amusing animal story in the bible is the tale of Balaam and his donkey. Read it in Numbers 22:27-30. Balaam is riding on his donkey when the donkey sits down. When it happens a second time, Balaam gives the donkey a beating. So the donkey gets up and they continue down the road. Suddenly the donkey sees an evil angel in the road. So the donkey sits down yet again. Balaam proceeds to flog the poor beast once more. Now for the good part. The donkey ASKS Balaam why he is beating him. And Balaam is not in the least nonplussed about the fact that his donkey can talk. In fact, he engages in an argument with the donkey, claiming that the animal has mocked him by sitting down. He informs the donkey that if he had had a sword, he would have killed him instead of beating him. The donkey argues that he has always let his master ride him, but never asked to ride his master. Balaam feels this is a good point and concedes defeat in the debate. What possible reason would God have for inspiring such a ridiculous story?

The book of Ezekiel is particularly strange. Ezekiel has a vision in which he purports to have seen four creatures called Cherubim, each having four faces (a man, an ox, an eagle, and a lion). As if that were not odd enough, each creature has human hands which are located under conjoined wings. Their feet are like brass and are connected to peg legs. Not only does Ezekiel see these bizarre creatures, he also gets a look at God. God is a golden color above his waist, on fire below the waist, and surrounded by a rainbow. (Ezekiel 1: 27-28) God takes an interest in Zeke. He orders him to eat a scroll. Zeke complies and says it tastes like honey. (3: 1-3) Then the Supreme Being decides he would like to toy with poor Ezekiel. God ties him up and sticks his tongue to the roof of his mouth. (3:24-26) The fun continues. God makes Zeke lie on his left side for 390 days and then his right side for 40 days. This is supposedly the number of years some regions lived in sin. (4: 4-6) You would think God would now give Ezekiel a rest. But no. God orders Zeke to bake a loaf of bread. Not so bad, but wait. He must bake it using human dung. Ezekiel balks at this and God relents. He may bake his bread using cow dung. After eating his lunch, Ezekiel is ordered to shave his head and divide the hair into thirds. God next tells him to

burn the first third, cut the second with a knife, and
scatter the third to the wind. After he has styled
his hair, Ezekiel must go to a location filled with
bones. God tells him to order the bones to assemble
themselves. Once they are assembled, the bones
become an army. (37:1-14). The bone soldiers declare
that they are constructed of dried bones and their
hope is lost. The book of Ezekiel has 48 chapters.
God devoted much time to him.

In Matthew 21:22 Jesus promises that if you
believe, anything you ask for will be given to you.
Of course this is not true. Apologists have said
that Jesus meant "as long as it is God's will". As
in most things related to religion, true believers
concoct excuses when errors are pointed out to them.
However, if they are correct in this case, there is no
point in praying because if it is not God's will, the
prayer will not be answered no matter how often you
pray.

In Exodus chapter 28, God becomes obsessed
with wardrobe. Be sure to read verses 33, 34, and 43
in which God threatens to kill Aaron if he does not
wear a golden bell and blue pomegranates. Again,
God seems to care about the oddest things while
neglecting major problems. Another Genesis gem is
found in chapter 18. Abraham has a picnic with God
and two angels. Read Genesis 32: 24-32 to discover
that Jacob wrestles with God. Who do you think wins
the match?

In Exodus 17:11 -12, the Israelites are engaged in
battle with the Amalekites. So long as Moses raises

both hands and keeps them raised, the Israelites are victorious. But if Moses gets tired and lowers his arms, the chosen people will lose the battle. So Aaron and Hur hold Moses' hands up for him until sundown and the Israelites prevail.

Read an horrendous story in II Kings 2:23-25. One of God's prophets is taking a walk when a group of children begin to tease him about his bald head. The prophet curses the children in the name of the lord, causing bears to come out of the woods and rip forty-two children limb from limb. That'll teach 'em.

Are we sure God inspired the holy bible, or was it Stephen King? And as for the bible being beautifully written, Shakespeare is looking better all the time.

Chapter 3

THE GREAT "US"

The universe is so majestic that it must have had a creator who created it just for us. There is no other plausible explanation.

The truth is that the very fact of the majesty of the universe demands an explanation more complex than "God did it."

If the universe was created by God, who created God? If your answer is that God has no beginning and no end, being eternal, I submit that the universe itself is eternal. "Ah, but the universe must have had a human-like being who created it. A watch has to have a watch-maker." This assumption is made because humans are by nature ego-centric. Everything that was and is and everything that happens and will happen has to be caused by a being resembling ourselves. Everything that exists has to have been made by such a being, and made for our benefit. A certain talk show host once said he knows

God exists because the moon exists. "Who PUT it there?" he shouted. Once again, there has to be an entity similar to the GREAT US responsible for all creation. Why is it more reasonable to believe that a mute and invisible god created everything than that the universe has evolved from an energy that has always been present?

The old testament account of creation came from the minds of simple men living in a simple age. Their god came down to earth and made everything in six days. He formed a man out of mud. He took a rib from him and made a woman. He said "Let there be light" and the sun magically appeared. He tacked stars onto the sky as you might notes on a bulletin board. He created a flat earth, as biblical references to the four corners of the earth and people falling off the edge assert. He created seven flat skies and walked about on the seventh one, opening sluice gates when he wanted to water the earth with rain. Hence the reference to seventh heaven. Amazingly, the Catholic encyclopedia acknowledges these biblical errors but tells us we have to consider the time in which the bible was written. Didn't God inspire every word in the bible? Surely he knew the earth was round, there are not seven layers of flat sky, and clouds cause rain. If we do indeed need to consider the time in which the bible was written, we must concede that an all-knowing god did not inspire it.

Over time humans have elevated the simple iron-age god to a deity who knows every thought every human being living on the earth has. This god can listen to the prayers and read the thoughts of millions of people simultaneously. He cares whether or not your football team wins the Super Bowl. He cares deeply about your private sex life and what foods you eat. He knows the exact moment every human was born and when he or she will die. He can turn himself into a burning bush, raise the dead, massacre thousands of men, women, and children on a whim, and condemn millions to eternal fiery torment just for questioning his existence.

Thankfully, in the past there were rational men who were centuries ahead of their time.

Heraclitus (535-475 BCE): "The universe has been made neither by gods nor man; but it has been, and is, and will be eternal."

Lucretius (94-49 BCE): "All religions are equally sublime to the ignorant, useful to the politician, and ridiculous to the philosopher. Nature is seen to do all things spontaneously of herself without meddling by the gods."

Anaximander (610-543 BCE): "Living creatures rose from the moist elements evaporated by the sun. Man was like another animal, namely a fish, in the beginning."

Buddha (623-543 BCE): "Do not believe in anything simply because you have heard it or it has been handed down for many generations, or because it is found written in your religious books, or merely on authority of your teachers or elders. Doubt everything, find your own light."

Anaxazoras (500-428 BCE): "Mind cannot arise alone without body or apart from sinews and blood. You must admit that when the body has perished there is an end to the spirit diffused throughout it. It is surely lunacy to couple a mortal object with an eternal one."

Regiomontanus (1463): "The common astronomers of our age are like credulous women, receiving as something divine and immutable whatever they find in books, for they make no effort themselves to find the truth."

How awesome is it that these men were able to come to their conclusions without the aid of Darwin or modern science?

What then is the alternative to God? How did the world as we know it come to be? Because of our flawed intellect, we tend to think there must always be a beginning to everything. But the religious consider God as having no beginning, having always existed. Consider that some things have always been, and those things are not gods, but matter and energy. When matter compacted and exploded the Big Bang occurred, sending said matter into the universe and eventually creating billions of planets and stars. An orbit called the Goldilocks Zone, so named because conditions are just right, happens to surround the earth. Our orbit is not so close to the sun to allow our planet to boil, and not so far away as to cause it to freeze. The orbit the earth takes is circular so that it never strays from the Goldilocks Zone. Scientists recently have discovered that other planets might

also fall into their suns' Goldilocks Zone. What
we must keep in mind is that that does not mean
an evolution to life occurred there. Even if it did
happen, evolution would not have occurred exactly as
evolution on earth did.

Every atom in a human body, with no exception,
was created in a carbon based star billions of years
ago in the aftermath of the Big Bang. As Carl Sagan
put it: "We are star stuff." You are here because of an
explosion that occurred many billions of years ago.
Every animate and inanimate thing that exists in the
universe, including us, consists of the same elements
as the planets and stars. We are star stuff!

The difference between science and creationism
is that for science to form a theory, facts must be
painstakingly tested and retested. Only when the
most stringent criteria is met successfully again and
again is a theory named a scientific theory. Gravity
is one such scientific theory, as are the germ theory
of disease and evolution. Gravity, germ theory and
evolution are fact. Creationists accept as fact what
is written in an ancient book by unknown ancient
people. Biblical claims are not doubted or contested.
When religious beliefs are proven inaccurate,
believers attempt to mold bible teaching to fit the
established facts. For example, the bible says the
earth is flat. But we need to consider the time in
which the bible was written. God is all-knowing, so
we surely do not. Fossil evidence proves the earth is
older than 6000 years. But Satan planted the evidence
to lead us away from God. Science starts with the

facts and determines if they fit the conclusion. If they do not, the facts are discarded. Creationism twists the facts to fit scripture.

The odds of something similar to a DNA molecule landing on our planet is extremely unlikely, but there are billions of planets in our galaxy, and billions of billions of galaxies in the universe. Entertain the possibility that such an event happened on at least one of those infinite number of planets.

Do not mistakenly conclude that evolution began with the ultimate intention of producing us. For life as we know it to evolve required a series of particular events that led to our being here, but those events could have easily transpired in a very different way. Consider for example the collision that wiped out the dinosaurs. If asteroids hadn't smashed into earth in prehistoric days and obliterated the dinosaurs, life would have evolved quite differently. We most probably would not be here. We are here because the smallest life forms lived burrowed under the earth in order to avoid the giant reptiles, and coincidentally survived the asteroid collision. Their survival and adaptation over time was essential to the progress of evolution.

The history of life here on earth is found in our fossils and rock layers. We have many fossils that show how species have come and gone over the last several hundred million years. In rock layers that are found at the deepest levels, no fossils are found. Above those layers are found simple bacteria and invertebrates. In the next level of rock, vertebrate fish are found. When primitive reptiles appear in rock formations, there are no mammal or bird fossils. When the first mammals do appear, they are small and rodent-like. Modern mammals are not found with these early fossils. When ancient hominids are found, there are no modern human fossils. You will never find people with dinosaurs or dinosaurs with trilobites. There are no fossils found out of order. Every species is a transition to the next. How much clearer could it be? The fossil record mirrors the genetic record. In other words, DNA testing shows the relationship among fossil remains in differing rock layers. There is NO other explanation for this relationship between DNA and fossils besides evolution. For the evolution from simple life forms to modern humans to take place, hundreds of millions of years must pass. Radiometric dating methods such as Carbon14 are the means by which we know that the earth is incredibly old. The claims that these methods are unreliable is untrue. (information found at evolution-for- beginners.html).

Seventy percent of the earth's surface is covered by water. Scientists have surmised that an additional 25 percent of water was present at the dawn of time. Human embryos have the remains of ancient gills. We were at one time in our distant past, fish. Archeologists have discovered remains of an ancient fish showing skeletal beginnings of hands complete with finger bones. Two excellent living examples of the journey from water to land are lungfish and mudskippers. Mudskippers are fish, but spend some of their lives out of water. They have gills, but when they emerge from the water, the gills dry up and stick together. While on land, they have highly modified front fins which they use like legs. Instead of swimming, mudskippers use their fins to simulate walking - on land and under the water. Lungfish are so named because they are able to breathe air when oxygen supplies are low in freshwater. Lungfish also have scrawny fore and hind limbs that allow them to elevate their bodies off the surface and move themselves forward. Walking has been seen to occur when they alternate their limbs and place each footfall in front of the other. The information concerning mudskippers and lungfish was able to be gathered only because scientists have observed the living animal. Fossil remains would not have revealed these fascinating facts.

Humans have a tail bone, a reminder of the ancient past when we did have tails. Why do our knees bother us at times? We have evolved from walking on all fours to walking upright. A certain tribe living in a remote area spends more time in the water than on land. They can hold their breath under water longer than the most expert swimmer. Scientists wondered why Himalayan sherpas were able to climb to great heights without the aid of oxygen tanks. An examination of the upper lips of the sherpas showed they had evolved more capillaries carrying blood and oxygen to the brain than ordinary people. When exposed to too many antibiotics, bacteria evolve an immunity and require alternative medicine. These examples show life forms changing over time to adapt to their environment. That is the definition of evolution.

My admittedly unscientific understanding:

1. Matter in the universe compacted and exploded causing the Big Bang.
2. Swirling matter compressed, forming stars and planets.
3. The Milky Way galaxy was formed.
4. Earth happened to fall into a Goldilocks Zone which is amenable to life.
5. Matter similar to DNA fell to earth.
6. Bacteria formed. From this humble beginning, all life evolved.

The biblical account presumes that Earth is the center of the universe. God created everything on and above the earth in order to accommodate the GREAT US. In fact, the bible says everything revolves around the earth. We are the center of the universe and the environment was created to serve us. The truth is that the environment was here long before humans made an entrance. The environment was not made to adapt to us. Through evolution, we adapted to it. Take the white polar bear. At one time all bears were brown, even those that lived in frigid temperatures. Because a gene malfunctioned, a white bear was born. That white bear thrived because she had a natural camouflage to allow her to get closer to prey. Eventually she produced a cub with the same coat color. The white cubs reproduced and continued the mutation in some of their offspring. They were able to consume most of the prey. Brown bears eventually died out. Darwin's Galapagos finches had differently shaped beaks because they evolved in the same way. Food source was different according to which island they lived on. Long slender beaks were found on the finches who needed to access food found deep under ground or buried beneath tree bark. Strong, sturdy, curved beaks were found on the birds inhabiting the island on which seeds were the major food source. A mutation amongst the finches caused a few to be born having longer beaks (or shorter, curved beaks). Eventually the trait became dominant and those not possessing it died out due to inability to access food. The same principle applies to the long-necked giraffe. When ground vegetation became sparse, giraffes with longer necks could access tender leaves at the tops of trees. And so, just as with polar bears and finches, the animals lacking the adaptation died off while those with it mated with similar giraffes.

We must change our mind sets and admit that the environment was not created for us. The environment was here long before we made our entrance. Evolution is adaptation to the environment. We have eyes because there is light. We have ears because there is sound. We have lungs because there is air.

Don't buy it? Perhaps you subscribe to Nietzsche's theory as outlined in his work "The Antichrist".

"The old God, wholly spirit, wholly the high-priest, wholly perfect, is promenading his garden. He is bored and trying to kill time.

Against boredom even gods struggle in vain. What does he do? He creates man – man is entertaining. But then he notices that man is also bored. God's pity for the only form of distress that invades all paradises knows no bounds, so he forthwith creates other animals. God's first mistake – to man these other animals were not entertaining. He sought dominion over them, he did not want to be an "animal" himself. So God created woman. In the act he brought boredom to an end and also many other things. Woman was the second mistake of God – woman is at bottom a serpent. Every priest knows that from woman comes every evil in the world. Ergo she is also to blame for science. It was from woman that man learned to eat from the tree of knowledge. The old God was seized by mortal terror. Man himself had become his biggest blunder. He had created a rival to himself. Science makes men godlike. It is all up with priests and gods when man becomes scientific. Moral – Science is forbidden! Science is the first of sins, the germ of all sins, the Original Sin! This is all there is of morality - "Thou shalt NOT know". God's mortal terror, however, did not prevent him from being shrewd. How is one to protect oneself against science? For a long while this

was the capital problem. Answer – out of paradise
with man! Happiness and leisure foster thought,
and all thoughts are bad thoughts. Man must NOT
think! And so God invents distress, death, the mortal
dangers of childbirth, all sorts of misery, old age,
decrepitude, and sickness. Nothing but devices for
making war on science. The troubles of man don't
allow him time to think. Nevertheless the edifice of
knowledge begins to tower aloft, invading heaven,
shadowing the gods. What is to be done? The old
God invents war, he separates the peoples, he makes
men destroy one another. (Priests have always had
need of war). War, among other things, is a great
disturber of science. Incredible!! Knowledge and
deliverance from the priests prosper in spite of war!
So the old God comes to his final resolution: "Man
has become scientific. There is no help for it. He
must be drowned."

Chapter 4

GOD LOVES US

Truth: God does not love women.

The bible was written BY men FOR men. There can be no doubt about it. The very first pagan deities were female for the simple reason that men didn't understand the birth process. The swelling of the female body and the subsequent appearance of offspring was considered a magical gift from a goddess who hatched the universe from an egg. When men discovered they were an integral part of reproduction, they usurped control by replacing the goddess with warrior gods and demoting women to undesirable status.

The authors of the bible were especially disgusted by women, a disgust driven by feelings of sexual lust which they didn't understand and couldn't control. To the primitive iron-age men who wrote the old testament, women were possessed with evil, satanic power. How else could they arouse such animal-like feelings in men? The writers supposed all evil began with women, thus the adoption of the concept of sin. Sin was the name of the Babylonian moon goddess, so of course all evil (sin) is female in origin.

God is morbidly obsessed with sex and the supposedly corrupt nature of women, as the following passages show:

Deuteronomy 25:11 says that if any man is engaged in a fight with another man and is losing, his wife may not grab him by the genitals in order to save him. If she does, her hand must be cut off.

Men should not touch women according to 1 Corinthians 7:1.

The bible encourages men to maintain vigilance in their search for the "tokens of virginity" in women. If after an exhaustive search these tokens are not found, the women should be stoned to death. This search is mentioned over and over again in the bible. It raises all sorts of unpleasant images. Virginity seems to be the overriding attribute for women. For men, not so much.

2 Samuel 12:11, Jeremiah 8:9, and Zachariah 14:1 all have something in common. All three passages tell of how God will give the wives of men away to be raped if the men do not obey his laws. God punishes men by having their wives raped. The women are cast off like the worthless possessions they are.

Genesis 3:16 says the lord wants to cause women great pain in childbirth, but not so much pain as to decrease desire for their husbands. This is supposedly for eating from the tree of knowledge and tempting Adam to do the same. Note how the Lord takes care of the men in this one.

If the daughter of any priest dares to go whoring, she is profaning her father and must be burned alive. It doesn't matter if she profanes herself, but how dare she profane her father? He is, after all, male. (Lev 21:9)

Moses leads the children of Israel against the Midianites in Numbers 31. You must read verses 9-18 for yourself. Moses tells his army to take all the women and children alive. Every male child is to be killed, and likewise every woman who is not a virgin. They are to keep for their own pleasure all virgins and female children.

Leviticus 12 says new mothers are unclean for one week after the birth of a male, and two weeks after the birth of a female. A new mother must undergo a purification ritual. If she doesn't, she might contaminate men. This not only involves isolation, she need also pay priests for the various rites they must perform in order to take away the "unclean" nature of childbirth. One of these is the ritual burnt offering, which supposedly helps to cleanse the woman of her impurities. How interesting that the new testament describes how even Mary herself was required to leave a burnt offering after the birth of Jesus. (Luke 2:24)

There is a ridiculous warning in Leviticus 15:19-33. It contains eleven verses telling men and women how to cope with menstruation. Read it to discover how many times men must wash themselves and whatever the woman sits upon to be free of the uncleanness, and what women must do to likewise cleanse themselves. The cleansing ritual also orders the woman to take either two turtles or two pigeons to the priest so that he may offer them up to God, one being a burnt offering and the other a sin offering. A sin offering is necessary because the woman must atone to God for her uncleanness.

Jesus Christ in Revelation 2:22-23 punishes women by murdering their children, but men can save themselves by repenting.

The following is one of the most thoroughly disgusting stories in the bible:

An angry mob tries to get a man to come out of the house he is staying in with his concubine. The mob shouts loudly that they wish to have their way with the man, but the homeowner comes up with an alternate plan: He generously offers up his daughter and his guest's concubine. When the mob insists upon having their way with the man, the guest takes his concubine out to them and they relent. They abuse her all night long and let her go in the morning. So the concubine suffers a long night of gang rape, but that's not all. In verse 26 we find that the poor woman collapses at the doorstep where she lays until the next morning when her "lord" opens the door and sees her. What does the homeowner do when he finds out? The only thing he can do- she is, after all, contaminating his threshold. He takes her

43

into his house, takes out a knife, and hacks her into twelve pieces. He then tosses her body parts into "all the coasts of Israel". (Judges 19: 24-29)

1 Corinthians 7:4 teaches that a wife is allowed no control over her own body- that privilege belongs to her husband.

Wives are ordered to submit to their husbands in all matters in 1 Peter 3:1

The lord is portrayed as a sexual pervert in Isaiah 3:17 when he threatens to publicly display the "secret parts" of the daughters of Zion.

Timothy 2:11 adamantly orders women to be silent and submissive. Why? Because God formed Adam first and Adam was perfect until Eve came along and allowed herself to be deceived. Because of this, she is the transgressor.

It's shameful for a woman to talk in church. If she wants to know anything, she should ask her husband. (1 Corinthians 14-34)

Jesus says in Revelation 14:4 that men who are not defiled by women may follow the lamb.

Why were Catholic women once required to cover their heads in church? Saint Paul in the first century of the common era gave this explanation: the tresses of women would arouse lust in the angels. That explains the headgear nuns used to wear. As an aside, the bible says that all angels are male. (See 'Snippets') Men need not cover their heads because they were created in the image of God, and God likes to see them in all their glory. If a woman dares to pray without a head covering, she must have her

"tresses shorn". Those angels are a lusty lot. The
bible also says that God does not approve of men
with long hair because they look too much like
women. Apparently, artists' depictions of Jesus and
the angels are offensive to God.

There are many more examples of the loathing
biblical authors had for women. This hatred led
to many centuries of brutal abuse, and in many
cultures the abuse continues. Let's look at some of
the comments of churchmen, many of whom were
canonized as saints.

"Do you not know that you are each an Eve?
The sentence of God on this sex of yours lives in
this age: the guilt must of necessity live too. You
are the Devil's gateway: you are the unsealer of the
forbidden tree: you are the first deserter of the divine
law: you are she who persuaded him whom the devil
was not valiant enough to attack. You destroyed so
easily God's image, man. On account of your desert
even the Son of God had to die." (St Tertullian of the
period of 155-225 CE)

"What is the difference whether it is in a wife
or a mother, it is still Eve the temptress that we
must beware of in any woman. I fail to see what use
woman can be to man, if one excluded the function
of bearing children." (St Augustine of Hippo 354-
430 CE)

"As regards the individual nature, woman is
defective and misbegotten, for the active force in
the male seed tends to the production of a perfect
likeness in the masculine sex, while the production

of woman comes from a defect in the active force or from some material indisposition, or even from some external influence. A woman is an imperfect male, something that is not intended in itself, but originates in some defect. Women do not correspond to nature's first intention, which aims at perfection (a man), but to nature's second intention which is (in woman) decay, deformity, and the weakness of age." (St Thomas Aquinas – a thirteenth century Catholic theologian) This same man actually said "Women find it harder to resist sexual pleasure since they have less strength of mind than men."

"We hereby proclaim women to be human." (Council of Nicea, 325 CE Conference of Christian Bishops) The declaration passed by a single vote.

"If women become tired or even die, that does not matter. Let them die in childbirth, that is why they are there." (Martin Luther (1483-1546)

"We are born between shit and piss." (St Augustine) Lovely.

"Women are a tool of Satan and a pathway to hell." (St Jerome)

Tertullian called women "a temple built over a sewer".

Marcion denied that his celibate god was the creator of "the disgusting paraphernalia of reproduction"

The saints Ambrose and Augustine believed that someone as clean as Jesus could not have come out of something so filthy as a female orifice, but must have magically appeared outside Mary's body. Even today, the Catholic church insists that Mary remained an intact virgin even after Jesus' birth.

Many saints received canonization by repressing the disgusting desires of the flesh. St Jerome (in his own words): "I lived in the desert amid scorpions and wild beasts until my skin was dry and my frame gaunt from fasting and penance, my body that of a corpse. All this was done in order to quell the cravings of desire and the fire of lust that burned in my flesh." John of Lycopolis intentionally banned all women from his sight for 48 years. Ammonius burned himself repeatedly with a hot iron. Mary Magdaline dei Pazzi suffered an hallucination telling her to roll around on thorns and whip herself. Simeon wore an iron belt that cut into his flesh. One might think all belonged in an asylum, but instead all were canonized.

At the seventh-century council of Nantes, the bishops declared in their third canon that women were soulless beasts given to men by God to use in whatever fashion they saw fit. They also determined that immortality was reserved for men only.

Even today Orthodox monks living an isolated life on the European peninsula of Mount Athos are adamant that the presence of a woman would defile the entire peninsula. Their fear and exclusion of females extends even to female animals.

But what about the Virgin Mary? It is true that she is prayed to and venerated as often as God or Jesus. But this is the result of purely human desire. Nowhere in the bible is it suggested that she be the object of prayer. The catholic encyclopedia says that she is mentioned but infrequently in the bible. She is never portrayed as one who can perform miracles, answer prayers, etc. She is presented as the mother of Jesus, and is only of interest because the story needed God's son to be born of a mortal woman.

The traditional teaching of the Catholic Church on the subject of souls: Male embryos acquire a soul 40 days after conception. Female embryos have to wait 80 days for their souls to materialize. We are discriminated against even as embryos.

Many of the religious point to the books of Ruth and Esther and try to make them more important than they are.

The book of Ruth is a mere three and a half pages long. The author is unknown. It's a silly story of a woman who took care of her mother-in-law, and was purchased to be the wife of a man whose grain she had "gleaned". The popular quote "whither thou goest" can be found in the book of Ruth and refers to her devotion to her mother-in-law. She was a meek woman (a quality much admired by the bible) who did nothing extraordinary at all, unless you think sleeping at the feet of her master was extraordinary.

A bit more time is devoted to the tale of Esther- about six pages. The story contains no mention of or referral to God. Why is it even in the bible? Only to denote the Jewish holiday of Purim. King Ahasuerus of Persia lived in Shushan Palace with his queen, Vashti. In the third year of Ahasuerus's reign, he hosted a magnificent party and drank royal wine from a golden goblet. When he was feeling a little merry from all the wine, he ordered his wife to appear at the gala so he could show her off to his guests. Apparently, Vashti wasn't in a party mood and refused to appear. Horror of horrors! What if all the wives in the kingdom got wind of Vashti's defiance? Why, they might think they too could defy their husbands. To prevent this from happening, the king's henchmen arranged to have all the virgins in the kingdom gathered up so that Ahasuerus could banish Vashti and select a new queen. The virgins took turns "visiting" Ahasuerus, but only after twelve months of purification. (How filthy were the women that they needed an entire year to be clean enough for their visits to Ahasuerus? And how were they cleaned? Disgusting images abound.) As you might guess, Esther was one of the lucky virgins. The king selected her and made her the new queen. What the king didn't know was that she and her father Mordecai were Jews. The king had a royal vizier, Haman. Haman planned to kill all the Jews in the kingdom and overthrow the king. There follows a tale in which Esther and her father saved the king by getting wind of the plot against him. When they told him about Haman's treachery, the king allowed them to form marauding bands to kill all the enemies of the Jews. Mordecai and his followers end up killing five hundred men in the palace, and seventy-five thousand in neighboring provinces. Thus ends the bloody and perverted tale of Esther.

The book of Esther is the basis for the Jewish holiday Purim. This fictional story (categorized as such by Jewish historical records) was written by an unknown author during the 3rd or 4th century BCE. It was written for the Jews living in exile in Persia. The book of Esther is indeed fiction. Details of the Persian culture are inaccurate and there exists no historical evidence to support a claim of the Persians wanting to kill all the Jews in Persia.

According to those who still attend Mass and church services, the majority of the faithful are women. I find that quite sad. Why are women so enthralled with religion, even seeming more susceptible than men? Just like their preferred books and movies, they always want the happy ending. Innocent children who die should float up to heaven and become angels. The fact that the bible contradicts that pleasant image doesn't seem to matter. Women want a god to love and protect them, even though the God of the bible clearly has nothing but disgust for them. They want guardian angels, miracles, answers to prayers. Deceased loved ones should be smiling and looking down at them on all their special occasions, even though the bible at one point says no one ascends to heaven until the second coming. But the fact is that most people don't read the bible, they fabricate their own truth the way they want it to be.

And let's be honest. Women are more likely to get caught up in the pageantry, the songs, the familiar repetitious responses to the rehearsed ramblings of priests and clergy. Bow, kneel, pray, sing, genuflect, talk to the rosary, light a candle, dab some holy water, take communion. It's all comfortable ritual. After a lifetime of this, it doesn't seem to matter if it's based on truth or not.

But one stark reality is that there are no women in the upper echelons of the Catholic Church. Protestants are making some gains, but only recently. If the holy bible detested men the way it detests women and totally rejected them in leadership roles, men would leave the faith in droves!

There is now talk of the possibility of the Catholic Church allowing priests to marry at some point. Why have they been expected to remain celibate all this time? It's been said it's because they must be free of the distractions of wife and family so that they can better tend to their sacred duties. Nonsense. It's because women have been portrayed in the bible as untrustworthy, evil, and inferior. Men who are untainted with the wiles of women are more holy and better suited for the church.

If you are interested in reading for yourself the bible verses describing the degradations of women, you had better hurry. An NBC newscaster recently reported that efforts are underway right now to alter the bible in order to make it more gender friendly. Recently a summarized version of the old testament was published. (Chord – The Old Testament Condensed) The story of the raped and murdered concubine was, not surprisingly, omitted. The Leviticus 26-29 verses wherein God orders his people to eat their sons and daughters are also missing, along with many of the other disgusting passages. The newly elected Pope Francis is right now trying to soften much of the bigoted dogma of the Catholic Church.

What does the bible say about adding to or deleting from the holy writ? Only that God will send biblical plagues and toss us out of his kingdom should we dare to change one "dot or tittle".

Chapter 5

WHY BE SO MEAN?

Religion is a good thing. Why try to debunk faith? It makes people happy and it's a model for righteous living.

"The idea that a believer is happier than a skeptic is no more to the point than that a drunken man is happier than a sober one." (Bernard Shaw)

The truth is that religion does not make people moral. Blind faith is dangerous. It's not true that atheism is responsible for abhorrent behavior; on the contrary, wars and discrimination throughout history have frequently had a religious component. Far from being a good thing, religion is a very dangerous thing when taken seriously. Whenever sanctimonious men impose their beliefs on others, free thinkers are vilified. Heresy used to be a capital offense; and believe it or not there have been in the past, and still are radicals out there who would love to see it reinstated as such.

"If my father were a heretic, I would personally gather the wood to burn him." (Pope Paul IV 1476-1599)

"The death penalty is a necessary and efficacious means for the church to attain its ends when obstinate heretics disturb the ecclesiastical order. Humanity is destined to remain as it is. The equal toleration of all religions is the same as atheism." (Pope Leo XIII)

While the following people may not have come right out and advocated murder, they certainly have had (and still have) interesting viewpoints.

"Reason is the devil's harlot." (Martin Luther)

"We sacrifice the intellect to God." (Ignatius Loyola)

"Hell was made for the inquisitive." (St. Augustine of Hippo)

"We hereby declare women to be human." Oh, what a relief! We didn't know what species we were until the august Council of Nicea told our ancestors back in 325 CE. And we made it into the human race by the margin of only a single vote.

"The bliss of the elect in heaven would not be perfect unless they were able to look across the abyss and enjoy the agonies of their brethren in eternal fire." (Pope Gregory the Great 540-604)

"From the polluted fountain of that absurd and erroneous doctrine, or rather raving, which claims

and defends liberty of conscience for everyone...
comes, in a word, the worst plague of all – liberty of
opinion and free speech." (Pope Gregory VI)

When Galileo dared to suggest that the sun did
not revolve around the earth, but in fact the earth
revolved around the sun, he was charged with heresy.
In 1632 Francesco Niccolini wrote a letter to the
pope. "I humbly begged His Holiness to agree to
give him (Galileo) the opportunity to justify himself.
Then His Holiness answered that in these matters of
the Holy Office the procedure was simply to arrive
at a censure and then call the defendant to recant."
Understandably uncomfortable with the thought of
burning at the stake, Galileo recanted. It is said that
when he was forced to state that the earth did not
revolve around the sun he muttered under his breath
"but it does."

Why was it so important to think all heavenly
bodies revolved around the earth? Earth had to be
the center of all creation because Genesis said it
was. Adam and Eve were the pinnacles of God's
magnificent work, and everything else was created as
an afterthought for their comfort. Once again, we are
the GREAT US for whom everything was made. The
universe was built around us. The earth had to be the
center of the cosmos. "One Galileo in two thousand
years is enough." (Pope Pious XII)

Pat Robertson is the well known host of the
television show The Seven Hundred Club. He has
controversial opinions on such things as rights for
gays, planned parenthood, and the place of women

in the family. But nothing compares to his speech following the devastating 2010 earthquake in Haiti that killed thousands. According to him the Haitians made a secret pact with Satan, promising to follow him if he would free them from French influence. When God found out, he cursed them with one disaster after another. In Pat's own words - "true story".

Jerry Falwell proudly compares Christians to slaves and soldiers in that they are not allowed to question. If you believe in the separation of church and state, you are unwittingly advancing an idea invented by the devil himself to keep Christians from running the country. And if you are not a born-again Christian, you are a complete failure as a human being.

The Attorney General under George W Bush said that Bush was in the White House because God put him there.

A former archbishop of Canterbury said in the twentieth century that fear of the hydrogen bomb was irrational because all it could do would be to take us to another world where we would all be transferred eventually anyway.

Ronald Reagan's Secretary of the Interior once stated that he saw no need to protect the environment because the second coming was imminent.

Have you ever heard of Dominionism? I had been spared the knowledge until an article written by William Morrow appeared in the June, 2012 edition of the Tampa Bay Times. This is a Christian evangelical movement that openly seeks to gain control over government, business, education, and media. Sadly, they've found many adherents in Florida. A Canadian preacher named Todd Bentley attracted thousands nightly at his Florida revivals and has appeared on television and the internet. Bentley claims to have been to heaven where he chatted with Saint Paul. His mission: "To arm an armageddon-ready military force of young people with a divine mandate to physically impose Christian dominion on nonbelievers."

What do I have against religion? I'm afraid of the above mentioned zealots. If you believe, I mean REALLY believe every bit of the bible to be absolute orders from an absolute god, aren't you duty bound to forcefully impose his rule? Thank goodness most religious people don't really know what that book says because they don't read it. Religion refuses to question. The bible contains all the truth we need to know. Thinking and reasoning are taboo. Ignorance is the only thing that will lead you to salvation. Do not question-do not reason. Eve dared to attempt to gain knowledge by eating from the forbidden tree and from that day to the present women have been the bane of man's existence.

As for the connection between religion and morality:

Less than 1% of all inmates in federal prison are atheists.

93% of the National Academy of Sciences members are atheists.

Chapter 6

JESUS CHRIST WAS
THE FOUNDER OF CHRISTIANITY

The truth is that Christianity would never have gained a foothold were it not for the man commonly known as Saint Paul.

Paul was the founder of the Christian religion. He was not a contemporary of Jesus and therefore never met him other than in dreams and visions. It was Paul who espoused the doctrine of the Trinity along with eternal life, original sin, and judgment day.

The concept of original sin is contradicted by both Jesus and the old testament. Jesus says in Matthew 19:27 that the only thing necessary for salvation is to keep the commandments. God states in Ezekial 18: 20-22 that the sins of the father will not be visited upon the son. What Paul did was change the teachings of Jesus into a religion very similar to Greek mythology.

Paul's journey to becoming the founder of Christianity began with a supposed visit from the heavenly Jesus while on the road to Damascus. The book of Acts tells the story of Paul's conversion. We learn in Acts 9: 3-7 that Paul and his companions were traveling to Damascus when Paul saw a light from heaven, fell to the ground, and heard Jesus ask him why he was persecuting him. Paul's companions saw nothing, but thought they heard a voice.

Now we read a second version in Acts 22: 6-9 in which the same events transpire, only in this account the men who accompanied Paul thought they saw a light but heard nothing.

As if these two contradictory accounts were not enough, we have one more in Acts 26:14. This time Paul and his companions all fell down. My KJV contains a strange exchange in which Jesus tells Paul it is hard for him to "kick against the pricks". I have no idea what that means, but at any rate this time Paul and his fellow travelers all fell to the ground.

Jesus, if he ever existed, seemed to have no knowledge of the Pauline doctrine of the atoning death of a divine being. This rather fantastic claim was made FOR him by Paul in Acts 9:20. Paul developed the doctrines that were to become Christianity from earlier mystic religions along with some aspects of Judaism.

The book of Acts is required reading for those who want to know more about the founder of

Christianity. Read chapter 14 : 8-11 and discover that
Paul presents himself as divine and able to perform
miracles. Galations 2:20 tells us he believes he is
being crucified as Christ was.

Most Christians assume that Trinity doctrine
is unique to Christianity. What is the Christian
definition of the Trinity? The Father is God, the
Son is God, and the Holy Spirit is God, but they are
not three gods. Each of these entities is God, but
together they are one god. Huh? Paul instituted the
doctrine of the Trinity in John 1:7. But a text from an
ancient Hindu bible says, "The three gods, Brahma,
Vishnu, and Siva, say: 'Learn O devotee, that there
is no real distinction between us. What to you
appears such is only by semblance. The single being
appears under three forms by the acts of creation,
preservation and destruction, but he is one.' The
Hindu bible was composed 1400 years before Christ.
Plato also set forth his version of the trinity 400
years before Christ. His Greek trinity was made up
of Agathon the Father, Logos the Word, and Psyche
the Spirit. Modern day believers who even attempt to
understand the Christian Trinity are still befuddled
by its nature. How can one god be three persons?
The god of the old testament clearly was only one
god. In spite of all evidence to the contrary, most
religious leaders insinuate that the Trinity is doctrine
unique to Christianity and divinely bestowed upon
Paul. Most likewise insist that this Trinity has
existed for all time. It seems odd that God waited
until Paul's conversion to Christianity to enlighten

us. As for its uniqueness, we have St. Jerome telling us "All ancient religions believed in the Trinity".

Paul was also the man who told Christians it was no longer necessary to obey many of the old testament prohibitions and laws. How convenient that God himself told him in a vision. God changed his mind about sacred old testament teachings and chose to tell Paul rather than Jesus?

As for the common argument which states that the new testament must be true because some old testament prophecy is fulfilled in the new, I suggest another possibility is that Paul or someone inspired by him simply wrote new testament passages to make it look like prophecy had been fulfilled.

Paul was a fascinating personality, meeting danger and hatred everywhere he went. Following his conversion on the road to Damascus, he traveled extensively spreading his doctrine. In most of the towns he visited people were less than ecstatic to hear his message, his personality being that of a trouble-making and disagreeable complainer. This uncomfortable fact led to many attempts to murder him. He stirred up hatred and dissent in local synagogues, often causing him to flee for his life. In Damascus he spoke in a number of synagogues but had to escape to Jerusalem when an attempt was made on his life. In Jerusalem Grecian Jews tried to kill him, causing him to flee to Tarsus. In all places where Paul attempted to spread his doctrine, he was threatened and abused.

Why was Paul so unpopular? Aside from the fact that he was changing the nature of the unalterable old testament and concocting a new testament by claiming direct communication with the heavenly Jesus, Paul had a strange personality. He continued to have odd visions and claimed communication with God and Jesus even though such communication was not granted to the apostles. In Galations he says he is being physically crucified as Jesus was, and even asserts he has the marks to prove it. He claims to have visited heaven. It is known that he was ridiculed by some Christian groups, even leading to the assertion that he was insane. He was thought to suffer from epilepsy and seizures, purported by some to have caused him to fall off his horse on the road to Damascus; an event which led to his conversations with Jesus.

Some scholars think Paul knew his claims were fiction, but why would he state such falsehoods? Many speculate that rejection by his Jewish brethren led him to found a new religion and thereby find acceptance and fame. It's possible that he himself did believe Jesus spoke to him. Religious followers of the Christian faith no doubt suppose his writings contain sacred truth. It is said by some that Nero sentenced Paul to death by beheading. The bible is unclear as to the means, but scholars agree that he was executed in Rome.

What we know as fact is that Paul never knew an earthly Jesus. The Christian religion is based upon his visions and dreams. There is no evidence that

Jesus himself, if he ever lived, believed himself to be a divine savior. Paul is the man who portrayed Jesus as a savior and a miracle worker. Unlike most biblical figures, we do have enough historical information to know that Paul was a real person. What sort of person he was is left to the reader to decide.

Chapter 7

THE TEN CONFUSIONS

The Ten Commandments Are the Most Perfect Set of Laws Ever Written

The truth is that those laws commonly referred to as The Ten Commandments are not called The Ten Commandments in the bible. The truth is that there are at least three sets of so-called commandments.

The set of ten laws that are commonly called The Ten Commandments and found in Exodus 20 are listed below. These are the only ones that most people are familiar with, but they are not called the Ten Commandments in the bible.

1. Thou shalt have no other gods before me.
2. Thou shalt not make for yourself a graven image, or any likeness of anything that is in

heaven above, or that is in the earth beneath, or that is in the water under the earth.

3. Thou shalt not take the name of the Lord thy God in vain.
4. Remember the sabbath day.
5. Honor thy father and thy mother that thy days may be long upon the land.
6. Thou shalt not kill.
7. Thou shalt not commit adultery.
8. Thou shalt not steal.
9. Thou shalt not bear false witness.
10. Thou shalt not covet thy neighbors house, or his wife, or his manservant, or his maidservant, or his ox, or his ass, nor anything that is thy neighbors.

Numbers 1, 3, and 4 seem to be attempts by God to assuage his vanity. Reminders, in other words, that he is to be worshiped and adored at all times.

Number 2 is an absurd law. Almost everyone has occasionally drawn a picture or engaged in some sort of craft work. Is all art blasphemy? What about the "graven images" of the ten commandments enshrined on stone tablets and present outside some courthouses? Most of us treasure the arts and consider them to be a cornerstone of an enlightened society. Imagine life without art. It's a bleak picture. And has there ever been an institution more obsessed with holy images than the Catholic Church? The churches of Catholics are awash in statues, shrines, crosses, and pictures. Parishioners bow down in front of them and pray. Every other home in some neighborhoods has a statue of the Virgin Mary on the lawn. Creches abound at Christmas. Popes, cardinals, bishops, etc are weighted down with assorted bling. It's amazing how many saints there are (over three thousand) and many come with a personal statue, worshiped and prayed to by the faithful. How do Catholics get around the second commandment? By ignoring it.

3 through 9 seem okay. Who could argue that murdering, lying, stealing, and committing adultery are not good things to avoid? However, good people are forced to kill in wartime, and we have seen that the sacred lawgiver himself has engaged in countless obscene acts of butchery and murder. Fathers and Mothers are not always people one is comfortable honoring, and who has never said, "Oh my God!" (or worse)? The ladies may object to number 10 which lumps wives together with asses and oxen in the list of a man's possessions. It is futile to order us not to covet since everyone has at some time or another admired the possessions of others.

But surprisingly, the aforementioned list is never called The Ten Commandments in the bible. These words were only spoken orally by God to Moses on Mount Sinai. Nevertheless, these are the only teachings that made it into common acceptance. Perhaps because the official list is too ridiculous to expect believers to accept.

The bible story goes as follows: The familiar commandments were spoken orally to Moses on

Mount Sinai. The people anxiously awaiting Moses'
return from atop the mountain saw lightning and a
smoking Mount Sinai, but they saw no stone tablets
because Moses had none. He only repeated to them
orally what God had told him. These are the rules we
are familiar with.

Then Moses was called to the mountain a second
time where God gave him a different set of laws
which God himself did divinely inscribe on stone
tablets. But when Moses descended to deliver the
tablets to the people, he became incensed to see that
they were worshiping a golden calf. He lost his cool
and smashed the tablets, and so he had to trundle
back up the mountain.

On his third trip up the mountain, Moses was
again given laws written on stone tablets by the
finger of God. They are stated in Exodus 34:14-26. In
34:1 God tells us Moses had to make two new stone
tablets since he smashed the first ones. On these new
tablets God wrote his laws, officially calling them
The Ten Commandments. Interestingly, Dan Barker
in his book "Godless" lists the following as the
official written-in-stone ten commandments given to
Moses that day:

1. Thou shalt worship no other god.
2. Thou shalt make thee no molten gods.
3. The feast of unleavened bread shalt thou
   keep.
4. Six days thou shalt work, but on the seventh
   day thou shalt rest.

5. Thou shalt observe the feast of weeks.
6. Thrice in the year shall all your menchildren appear before the Lord God.
7. Thou shalt not offer the blood of my sacrifice with leaven.
8. Neither shall the sacrifice of the feast of the passover be left until the morning.
9. The first of the first fruits of thy land thou shalt bring unto the house of the Lord thy God.
10. Thou shalt not seethe a kid in his mother's milk.

1,2,and 4 are familiar. As for the feast of weeks and the feast of unleavened bread, they seem to apply to early Hebrews. It's unlikely that many people today would seethe a kid in its mother's milk, so we are safe there. Only the boys get to "thrice in the year appear before the Lord God". Where should they go? Once again girls are left out of God's plan. In any case, they need not concern themselves with this commandment.

The Supreme Being's purpose for these commandments is to relate to his creation his most sacred rules. These are of the utmost importance, requiring extreme punishment when not obeyed. Yet six of the ten have to do with food. There are no more important commandments than these?

My bible, which is the source for this book, is the King James Version. Here, word for word, is what appears in my bible as the official written in stone by

God ten commandments given to Moses on his third trip up the mountain: (also Exodus 34:14-26:

1. For thou shalt worship no other god, for the Lord, whose name is Jealous, is a jealous god.
2. Thou shalt make thee no molten gods.
3. The feast of unleavened bread shalt thou keep.
4. All that openeth the matrix is mine; and every firstling among thy cattle, whether ox or sheep, that is male.
5. But the firstling of an ass thou shalt redeem with a lamb; and if thou redeem him not, then shalt thou break his neck. All the firstborn of thy sons thou shalt redeem. And none shall appear before me empty.
6. Six days thou shalt work, but on the seventh day thou shalt rest.
7. And thou shalt observe the Feast of Weeks, of the first fruit of wheat harvest, and the feast of ingathering at the week's end.
8. Thrice in the year shall all your menchildren appear before the Lord God, the God of Israel.
9. Thou shalt not offer the blood of my sacrifice with leaven; neither shall the sacrifice of the feast of the passover be left until the morning.
10. Thou shalt not seethe a kid in its mothers milk.

Diane Rogers

It seems obvious that **Mr. Barker's** list is from one of the many revisions the holy bible has gone through. The authors have deleted the ridiculous fourth and fifth commandments found in my copy and broken the seventh commandment into three.

Chapter 8

HOLY FATHERS?

His Holiness, the Pope, is chosen by God to be his emissary on earth. Therefore the pope is infallible.

Truth: Throughout the history of the Roman Papacy, a great many popes have been anything but holy. As for infallible, history proves that they most certainly were and are not.

More than 1800 years had passed since the time of St Peter before church cardinals began to discuss papal infallibility. After several weeks of debate, they decided by majority vote that the pope is to be considered infallible. In 1870 the church declared that acceptance of the infallibility doctrine was necessary for salvation.

Popes are not mentioned in the bible. Catholics refer to the pope as the Vicar of Christ. Webster defines the word vicar as meaning: "one serving as a substitute or agent; one authorized to perform the functions of another in higher office." Thess. 2:3-4 says that any man who is exalted and presented as if he were God is a man of perdition. The words Holy Father are used only once in the bible and are used by Christ when referring to God. (John 17:11)

In 1837 Bishop John Purcell spoke before the Vatican Council and declared that he and many of his fellow bishops did not agree with any doctrine of papal infallibility. Nevertheless, the Vatican Council decreed that the pope is to be considered infallible.

Most Catholics have gone their whole lives believing that popes throughout history were chosen by God, and as such were to be loved, obeyed, and respected. Historically speaking, many of the popes have not been loved or respected. Conversely, they have been hated and feared. And deservedly so.

The utter arrogance astonishes. "The popes, like Jesus, are conceived by their mothers through the overshadowing of the Holy Ghost. All popes are a certain species of man-gods... all powers in heaven, as well as on earth are given to them." (Pope Stephen V) All of these pompous declarations are totally man-made, having no mention in the bible. As to their being beyond reproach:

Fifth century popes Innocent I and Gelasius I both said babies who died after baptism but before receiving communion would go straight to hell. Imagine the agony such a disgusting papal edict would cause for gullible parents. This view was later condemned by the Council of Trent. So much for infallibility.

In 897, Pope Stephen VI demonstrated his hatred of his predecessor, Pope Formosus by having his body exhumed and dressed in full papal regalia. He then ordered the body displayed on the throne in the Basilica of St. John Lateran in Rome. Stephen then interrogated the corpse in the debacle known as The Cadaver Synod of January 897. Stephen found the corpse guilty of being an "antipope", cut off two of its fingers and ordered the body tossed into the Tiber River. The body of Formosus was later rescued from the Tiber and re-buried. But poor Formosus was not long into his eternal rest when Pope Sergius III (904-911) ordered him dug up again. This time he had the body beheaded and three more of its fingers cut off. Once again, the body was tossed into the Tiber. Eventually the corpse was rescued from the Tiber and reburied. So far, there have been no additional exhumations.

Unhappy with his behavior and edicts, the followers of Pope Steven VIII cut off his ears and nose in the year 930.

Enter John XII (955-964) who became pope at age sixteen. A sexual deviant, he had sex with men, women, children, and even his own mother. In a further depraved act, he gave shows for large audiences in which he personally had sex with horses. While still in his twenties, he was beaten to death with a hammer by the jealous husband of one of his lovers. How in the world did such an obviously flawed man become pope? His father, a contributor to the wealth of Roman nobility, blackmailed nobles into swearing an oath that at the time of the next papal vacancy his son would be chosen.

Sometime around the year 964, Pope Benedict V was caught raping a young girl. He ran off to Constantinople, taking the papal treasury with him. When the money ran out, he returned to Rome where he was murdered by a jealous husband. (Incidentally, murder by a jealous spouse was the fate of more than one pope) An irate mob dragged his corpse through the streets of Rome, eventually tossing it into a cesspool.

Benedict IX (1032-1044, 1045, 1047-1048) was known for holding the office of pope three separate times! He was first elected at a very young age thanks to his father, a powerful politician who reserved the papacy ahead of time for him. Benedict performed his duties in a lackluster manner, perhaps because he devoted all his time to obscene acts of rape and murder. When he became interested in marrying his cousin, he sold his position as pope for a large sum of money to his godfather (who named himself Pope Gregory VI). When he reclaimed his position a third time, King Henry III of Germany intervened and Benedict was excommunicated. Pope Victor III said of him, "His life as pope was so vile, so foul, so execrable, that I shudder to think of it."

Gregory VI was known to have said, "From the polluted fountain of that absurd and erroneous doctrine, or rather raving, which claims and defends liberty of conscience for everyone comes, in a word, the worst plague of all – liberty of opinion and free speech."

Gregory VII (1045-1046) was the only pope to perform a quite unusual canonization. He canonized himself! He is also responsible for personally writing a list of the God-given powers of the papacy.

1. The pope cannot be judged by any mere human.
2. The church has never erred, nor will it ever err until the end of time.
3. The pope is the superior of all kings and emperors, and can dethrone any ruler at will.

Innocent III (1198-1216) is probably one of the better known early popes. The Oxford Dictionary of Popes says he was "a man born to rule, uniting exceptional gifts of intellect and character and also humaneness." The other side of that coin is that he believed devoutly in the Holy Crusades. Innocent is personally responsible for more murders than any other pope in history. He ordered the bloody massacre of hundreds of thousands in Southern France-either by sword or burning at the stake. As each report of victory was related back to Innocent, he encouraged the crusaders to go forth and find yet more heretics to murder.

Not satisfied with the degree of Innocent's religious fanaticism, Pope Gregory IX instigated the horror of the Inquisition. It took three hundred years for any pontiff to denounce this atrocity.

Clement VI (1342-1352) had a love for the good life. He raised taxes and engaged in graft to finance his sexual adventures and luxurious life style. In his own words: "My predecessors did not know how to live."

Pope Eugenius IV (1431-1447) condemned Joan of Arc as a witch and had her burned at the stake. Benedict XV elevated her to sainthood in 1920.

Sixtus IV (1471-1482) was overly fond of the lucrative practice of papal indulgences. In other words, he convinced the faithful that he alone, as God's emissary, could help their deceased loved ones who were burning in hell. For a price, of course. Sixtus was also responsible for beginning the Spanish Inquisition.

Alexander VI was the Borgia pope, considered to be the most vile of all the popes. Born Rodrigo Borgia, his uncle was Pope Calixtus III. Because of his enormous wealth and social status, Borgia was able to buy the papacy. He is known to have fathered at least seven illegitimate children and was fond of rewarding them with elaborate gifts, all at the expense of the church. One of his money making practices was to frame wealthy citizens with blatantly fabricated charges, execute or imprison them, and steal their money. Another scheme was to sell the position of cardinal to ambitious men for a large sum, poison them, and then repeat the cycle. He left the city of Rome in financial and moral ruin.

The future Pope Leo X stated after Borgia's election: "Now we are in the power of a wolf, the most rapacious perhaps that this world has ever seen. And if we do not flee, he will inevitably devour us all."

What about later popes? Pope Leo XIII as late as 1903 espoused the death penalty for heretics.

Pope Pius XIII (pope from 1939-1958) was notorious for his approval of the Holocaust. He spoke out in favor of amnesty for German war criminals. Infallibility? In 1979 Pope John Paul II admitted the fallible nature of the Papacy when he stated that the Pope in Galileo's time had been mistaken for saying that the earth was the center of the universe and the sun orbited the earth. In other words, Galileo had been correct all along. Mea Culpa for sentencing the seventy year old man to house arrest and threatening him with the horrors of the Inquisition.

Popes such as Paul III, Paul IV, Pius IX, and others called the Inquisition holy. They supported and endorsed wholeheartedly the murderous and heinous torture and death of so many innocent people. It wasn't until the twentieth century that the late Pope Paul II finally apologized for this crime against humanity. This same Pope admitted on October 22, 1996 that evolution is more than an hypothesis.

The current Pope Francis recently washed the feet of twelve elderly people, showing his willingness to serve like a slave. His intention was to promote his vision of the papacy as a more humble and service-oriented position. But traditionalist church officials were appalled by this show of humility. Why? Francis washed the feet of (gasp!) WOMEN. Their horror was triggered by the Vatican's own regulation that the ritual be performed only on men. Personally, I don't care because I wash my own feet.

Chapter 9

A MOTHER'S LOVE

Mother Teresa was a selfless and compassionate woman who devoted her life to the care of the sick and suffering.

The truth is that the worldwide adoration shown to this woman is entirely undeserved.

Mother Teresa (AKA Agnes Bojaxhiu) was staunchly opposed to birth control, even under extreme circumstances. When asked about her thoughts on ways to help the poor in a vastly overpopulated India she offered no suggestions, saying only that God would provide. Well, that obviously isn't true. Four hundred twenty million people living in India at the time of that statement were barely surviving and living in abject poverty.

Teresa was obsessed with the bizarre notion that human suffering was somehow beautiful. When a dying patient begged for pain killers, she was said to have told him that his agony proved that Jesus himself was kissing him. It seems that in a sadistic way she welcomed the suffering of the poor and had no desire to relieve it. Instead she actively encouraged it, declaring that shared suffering with Christ was a gift from God. When asked how the poor and destitute can endure such misery, she suggested they smile more.

People assumed their contributions were going to alleviate the suffering in India. In actuality her so called hospitals had no doctors or nurses, a very small supply of medicines, and no humane care to speak of. Critically ill people lay on mats on the floor, often times 50 or 60 in a room. The only medical care they received was from a few untrained nuns and brothers. There was one communal open toilet and a policy allowing no visitors.

Teresa received a million dollar contribution from convicted Savings and Loan swindler Charles Keating. And what did he want in return? Only her personal plea to the presiding judge for clemency. When this was uncovered, she was asked to return the money because it had been stolen by Keating in the first place. She never did. She also took money from Duvalier, the brutal dictator of Haiti. Duvalier had taken the money from the Haitian public treasury at a time when the Haitian people were starving.

She claimed to have 102 family assistance centers in Calcutta, but an extensive investigation revealed not one single such center.

So what was being done to justify the millions
in contributions? A spokesperson said that Teresa
was not interested in how much work was actually
accomplished, the only thing that mattered was
how much love was shown to those who suffered. So
results don't matter? The Mission of Charity is the
only Indian charity that refuses to allow anyone to
examine its books. In 1998 a former Missionaries of
Charities worker revealed that she had been assigned
by Teresa to help monitor the millions of dollars
acquired by the charity. She asserted that most of the
money sat unused in various bank accounts earning
enormous sums of interest for the Vatican while the
sisters had to go about begging local merchants for
food. Why? Teresa told them that poverty is beautiful.
If local tradesmen could not help out, the soup
kitchen was closed that day. One of her supporters
even admitted that wiping out poverty and illiteracy
was never one of Teresa's focuses. Just what was her
focus? One of her fans, Clark Morphew (a syndicated
columnist), declared that Teresa never intended to
offer medical care to the ill, feed the poor, or educate
the illiterate. Instead her only intention was to offer
spiritual solace to dying people. That seems like
something anyone could do. Just an occasional
prayer and an admonition to smile?

Was Teresa herself resigned to a beautiful life of
poverty and suffering ?

Of course not. She was too selfless to allow
herself to enjoy the kisses from Jesus reserved for
the suffering poor. When she encountered a medical

condition such as a need for a pacemaker implant or the clearing of a blocked blood vessel, she jetted off to a hospital. She was friendly with the likes of Princess Diana and the Reagans. She enjoyed flying first class to hobnob with them and raise more money. She was known for reserving only the finest accommodations for herself when traveling. As a matter of fact, she spent the majority of her time away from Calcutta with long stays at exclusive residences in Europe and the United States. She enjoyed jetting on private planes to Rome, London, and New York.

What did this Nobel prize winner say was the greatest threat facing world peace? Birth control of course, and abortion. She claimed that her mission fed over a thousand people daily. As time went on, she increased those numbers to 4000, 7000, and 9000. People who knew the inner workings of her Mission of Charity admitted that the soup kitchens fed no more than 150 people daily. Teresa claimed 5000 children as students in her school in the Calcutta slums. Documented actual enrollment - less than 100.

In a story covered very lightly by NBC news, an examination of her diaries in 2007 by Catholic authorities in Calcutta revealed some hidden truths about Teresa. Apparently the examiners were hoping to find uplifting and saintly comments which might aid in her beatification. What they found instead was the following: : "I feel that God does not want me, that God is not God and that he does not really exist. People think my faith, my hope, and my love are overflowing and that my intimacy with God and union with his will fill my heart. If only they knew. Heaven means nothing. I am told God loves me – and yet the reality of darkness and coldness and emptiness is so great that nothing touches my soul."

Why is it people have no idea of the truth about this woman?

Chapter 10

MIRACLES HAPPEN EVERY DAY

Truth: The validity of this statement depends on your definition of the word "miracle".

Is it an event so extraordinary that NOTHING but divine intervention can explain it? When you accept this definition, understand that never in all recorded history has an actual miracle taken place. The bible is not recorded history.

But if you define "miracle" more loosely as an unlikely event with God's possible involvement, you are assuming that events that occur rarely must be a result of God's intervention. Let's examine this definition, the one the faithful always put forth as proof of God. You pray that you will survive a dangerous surgery. You do in fact survive. But you would not have survived without the expertise of surgeons. If you believe so devoutly in miracles, why didn't you just pray for a recovery and skip the surgery? If that seems extreme, remember that thousands of the devout do not survive surgery even though they had as many prayers as you. Why were they denied a miracle? A pilot lands a plane in the river and no one is hurt. It's called Miracle on the Hudson. The same plane in the hands of someone other than a skilled pilot would probably result in disaster. Even if an untrained pilot landed the plane successfully; it's a rare occurrence, not a miracle. There need be no divine intervention for these events to take place.

Why would people call such events miracles, insinuating that they couldn't have occurred without the intervention of God? Of course they could. And there are things that a god could do which would truly be called miraculous. Why doesn't he? God can do anything, so why do all the miracles have to be events that can easily be explained by means other than divine intervention? Diagnosed with a fatal disease for which there is no hope? If you do survive, it's because of a fluke or a misdiagnosis. Think of the millions of people who are likewise diagnosed, pray as fervently as you, and never the less die from their afflictions. But take the example of regrowth of missing limbs. God heals a cripple. He can miraculously walk again. If this isn't simply a case of excellent rehabilitation or the body healing itself, why can't God regrow legs that have been blown off by a roadside bomb? A beloved family member is cremated and the urn is buried. The family prays and the deceased rises from the ashes fully restored in front of many witnesses. She is returned to her normal life. Ridiculous you say? Why? God and assorted saints can do anything, and yet they choose to perform miracles that can easily be explained as nothing but coincidence. And the miracles required for elevation to sainthood? Shouldn't they be of an exceptional quality? They aren't, they're as commonplace as ordinary miracles.

Miracles are a necessary component of the Catholic process of canonization, the elevation to sainthood. It's laughable the extreme to which the church will go in order to canonize individuals, including badgering hapless civilians into declaring that they prayed to a picture or statue and were miraculously cured of a disease. The church has done away with the use of a Devil's Advocate, someone who would point out problems with declaring an event a miracle. Why have they eliminated this step in the canonization process? I surmise it is because they have never, and will never, prove divine intervention.

In 1969 Malcolm Muggeridge and his camera man Ken Macmillan traveled to India and while there attempted to film Mother Teresa's Home for the Dying. Even though it was very dark inside, Macmillan was able to film the interior showing every detail. Muggeridge proclaimed it a miracle and promoted Mother Teresa until she became world famous. But it was suggested that direct testimony from the cameraman might be more reliable than Muggeridge's miracle claim. Macmillan stated that the photograph had been remarkable, but suggested the reason was more likely a new film produced by Kodak which he had not had time to test before the trip.

Mother Teresa died in 1997. One year later, nuns in Bengali stated they had placed a medal Mother Teresa had worn onto the stomach of a woman named Monica Besra who was suffering from what appeared to be a large tumor. The woman recovered and the miracle was celebrated as the one needed to put Teresa on the path to beatification. Upset by the claim, the three physicians who had treated Mrs. Besra came forward to say that the woman had been suffering from tuberculosis and an ovarian growth. Both conditions had been successfully treated. Dr. Ranjan Mustafi, Monica's gynecologist, became annoyed when he received numerous calls from the "Missionaries of Charity" (a Mother Teresa organization) badgering him to say that the cure had been miraculous. Mrs. Besra herself was poorly educated and begged to be excused from the incessant questioning. Her husband spoke up after a while and said that his wife had been cured by ordinary medical treatment.

But what does the bible say about miracles? There are three words used in the bible to define a supernatural as opposed to a natural event. They are miracle, sign, and wonder. You can find these terms in Acts 2:22, Hebrews 2:4, and Corinthians 12:12. Interestingly, and absent from present day miracles, the bible says that in order to be called a miracle

God would have to work totally outside the laws of nature. Therefore, we must not declare as miraculous an event that merely seems astonishing or unusual. Examples of non-miracles would be recovery from disease, avoidance of an accident, a successful surgery, etc. Biblical miracles were unmistakably supernatural events. Today's miracles fall very short of that. Biblical miracles included turning water to wine, raising the dead, ascension into heaven, the turning of a mortal woman into a pillar of salt, talking donkeys and snakes, parting of the seas, etc. etc. These miracles abound in the bible, but have never occurred outside the bible.

The single most ludicrous claim is that today's tongue speaking is a sign of a miracle. Saint Paul himself said that a person possessing ability to speak in tongues (ridiculous babble) was not spiritually superior to one with no such ability. (ICorinthians 14:6,9,12,19) The term "unknown" when it refers to speaking in tongues was italicized in the King James version of the bible because translators wanted to convey that the languages to which Paul referred were totally unknown to the speaker. The new testament recognizes only tongue speaking which is in a legitimate language and can be proven to be unknown to the speaker. The key word here is legitimate, meaning a recognized and real language of which the speaker can be proven to be previously unaware. Also, the speaker must address an audience that does know the language in order to verify the fact that the language is legitimate. Only then could the event be called a miracle. In other words, were I to suddenly speak in fluent Italian, it would be truly miraculous. The tongue-speaking of the bible was of real and used languages, not incoherent gibberish. Surely it's apparent that anyone can babble incoherently and wave her arms in the air while spinning around in ecstasy. We hear from Saint Paul in I Corinthians that any person speaking a language he does not know the meaning of will be a barbarian. He also said that tongue speakers must remain silent if no interpreter is present. So far no one has successfully met the new testament criteria for tongue speaking. And, might I add, no one ever will.

The bible says in Acts II that only the apostles can perform miracles. Since there are no apostles alive today, people who claim they are able to perform miracles are lying either to themselves or to the rest of us. The bible also says that miracles ceased at the close of the first century, due to God's revelation that believers should now have all the facts they need to know in order to live according to his will, and such facts are told of in his holy book. The curing of purely ordinary ailments like arthritis, headaches, influenza, etc. are not miraculous. Why aren't televangelists going into hospitals and instantly causing the brain tumors of terminal cancer patients to disappear? Why can't they instantly and magically drop food in front of the millions who are starving in this world?

I will examine two miracles declared as such by the Catholic Church, and one 'miracle in waiting'. The most celebrated is the Miracle of the Sun at Fatima in Portugal in the year 1917 during the First World War. Three children reported that they had been visited by the Virgin Mary several times while working in a field. She told them that a miracle would occur on October 13th of that year. Newspapers spread the word quickly and on that date thousands of miracle - seeking people from far and wide swarmed the field. There were rain clouds present that day and when the sun came out it appeared to dance, spin, and change colors. Photographs were taken and newspaper articles written. Thirteen years later, the Roman Catholic Church officially declared it a miracle.

How could it not truly be a miracle if so many people witnessed the same "sun miracle"? Two of the three children (aged 7 – 10) died of influenza within a couple of years. But the surviving child, Maria Santos, lived to be 97. During the year of the miracle, Maria's mother was interviewed. She said that her daughter was "a fake who is leading half the world astray". Friar Mario de Oliveira knew the family very well and stated that Maria lived in a world consisting of fantasies and suffered from hallucinations. But how did so many people see the same miracle of the sun? It seems obvious that a person would not travel hundreds of miles to see such a miracle if he/she were not already extremely religious. They were therefore desperately looking for something to be called miraculous. When a large number of people are staring intently at the sun and a few shout out that the sun is doing amazing things, I would think that sun blindness would take over and you would indeed think the sun was dancing and spinning. Try it sometime. I can't help but wonder why, if the virgin were trying to proclaim a miracle, she didn't simply APPEAR and talk to the throng gathered there.

And now an even more amazing part to the story. Maria claimed that the virgin had told her three secrets. Many years later Maria became a nun and in 1941 the Bishop of Leiria asked her to reveal the secrets. It turns out the first secret wasn't really a secret at all, but a vision of hell. The second secret was the prediction that World War I would end, and World War II would start if man persisted in annoying God. But wouldn't you know? World War II had already started when she disclosed her great secret. The third secret was sealed in an envelope marked "Do not open until 1960". In 1990 a Vatican spokesman said that the third secret was just a rambling vision of angels with swords, corpses, murdered priests and bishops, and souls rising to heaven.

Everyone has heard of the Miracles of Lourdes. In 1858 a young peasant girl named Bernadette Soubirous declared that the Virgin Mary had appeared to her some eighteen times in a grotto next to the river Gave in Lourdes, France. The message relayed by the virgin was "Pray and do penance for the conversion of the world, and drink of the spring water." In the past 150 years, more than 200 million people have traveled to Lourdes to drink the water and hopefully receive cures for various ailments. Not surprisingly, not a single one of the reported "miracle cures" have involved something such as regrowth of missing limbs. The Catholic Church has nevertheless declared 67 of the events at Lourdes miraculous cures. That's a success rate of .0000335%, or one out of 3 million. (Skeptic.com) Belgian philosopher Etienne Vermeersch stated that there are probably more fatal accidents suffered by pilgrims on the way to and from Lourdes than there have been cures. Bernadette was canonized and her body put on public display. (very creepy) The faithful say that her body is incorruptible and proclaim that to be a miracle in itself. But the face and the hands have been expertly coated in wax. The population of Lourdes is around 15,000. Five million tourists make the journey there each year. There are 270 hotels. Thrown about in the grotto are all manner of things – crutches, eye glasses, hearing aids, etc. etc. This led one doubter to wonder why there were no artificial limbs. Of course shops are prolific with statues, pendants, and all sorts of souvenirs. Perhaps you are unable to make the arduous journey. Do not despair. The good people of Lourdes will mail you a vial of the holy water direct from the grotto. For a price, of course. Just go on the internet and type in "Lourdes water".

The third is the Medjugorje so-called miracle. This event traces back to 1981, when six teenagers said they saw the Virgin Mary on a hill near their village in what was then part of Yugoslavia. She appeared surrounded by a white light and holding a baby. Mary motioned for them to approach. They were frightened and ran back to their village. When locals went to the spot, they saw nothing. But the same teenagers saw her again the next day, and this time the vision confirmed the fact that she was indeed the Virgin Mary. After that, the same individuals claimed that the identical vision appeared to them almost daily in different places over the next ten years, visible only to them of course. Huge crowds of miracle seekers always gathered, but saw nothing. The local priest was said to have concluded that Medjugorje would be the church's greatest embarrassment of the twentieth century. The Vatican has yet to validate the sightings as a miracle. But more than 30 million people have visited the area in the past 30 years. What do these three miracles have in common? They are all based on revelation! And it's revelation only to a select individual or group of individuals. Christianity, Islam, and Judaism offer the same flimsy foundation. Religion will never come up with a satisfactory answer for why its deities reveal themselves only to a select individual or small group of individuals and not to humanity as a whole.

Just ignore the second commandment (Thou shall not make for yourself a graven image, or any likeness of anything that is in heaven above, or that is in the earth beneath, or that is in the water under the earth) and worship statues and pictures that seem to weep, bleed, and come to life in some way. These icons seem to pop up from time to time. In 1981, a statue in California of Our Lady of Fatima was said to weep. An investigation revealed a hoax. All studies of such statues or pictures coming to life in some way have been outed as hoaxes, the results of "pious imagination" as one priest called them.

Very popular is the "blood of San Gennaro St. Januarius" in Naples. He was supposedly a martyr, but his actual existence as an historical figure has never been verified. His congealed blood (?) is kept in a sealed vial and will sometimes liquify and redden. Of course researchers have never been allowed to run tests on the said blood. Three Italian chemists have a theory, nevertheless. A gel made by mixing chalk and iron chloride with salt water will liquify when shaken and solidify when standing. Another theory proposed suggests that an oil and wax pigment mixture will liquify whenever the temperature increases. It's interesting that the blood does not require prayer or incantation and will often liquify on its own. The red color of the blood is due to light passing through the liquified substance, whatever it be. It's interesting to note that the Naples area has miraculously been the site of additional saints' blood liquifying. Not a small boon for tourism.

Probably the most famous of religious icons is the Shroud of Turin, a burial cloth said to contain

the image of the crucified Christ. Many of the
faithful still claim the image is that of Christ, even
though history has revealed that a forger admitted
to painting the image in the mid fourteenth century.
Problems with the image are that the "blood" is still
suspiciously red even though blood blackens with
time. Microscopic analysis shows traces of paint
pigment. The "blood" was found to be tempura
paint. Carbon dating on the cloth was done in 1988,
showing the cloth to be from the time period of
1260 – 1390.

Chapter 11

SNIPPETS

"God took my precious granddaughter because he needed another angel."

Truth according to scripture: Angels are not former human beings. They are mentioned over 108 times in the Old Testament and 165 times in the New Testament, providing plenty of explanation as to what they are. The bible says that all angels were created by God at one time. No new angels are being added and they never die. Angels never appear as infants and children. Angels never appear as female. They were all created at one time by God as fully grown young adult males and do not age. The function of angels appears to be as God's messengers. They are sometimes good and sometimes evil. They do not require wings, and references in the bible say nothing about these appendages. In fact, they are often mistaken for humans when they appear on earth. Nowhere in scripture does it say that an individual is assigned a personal angel to protect her/him. The idea of guardian angels began with the Jews sometime in the period between the formation of the old and new testaments. Some early Christian leaders even developed the idea that not only does each individual have a guardian angel all his own, he also has a personal demon. Even though the idea of guardian angels has been around for a long time, there is no explicit scriptural mention of them. Scripture says God may send an angel to help an individual at times, but said angel is not assigned permanently to that particular person.

The bible does mention seraphim and cherubim, which some people mistakenly call angels. Seraphim are described as divine beings superior to angels whose sole purpose seems to be to fly above God's throne and sing non-stop for all eternity, "Holy, holy, holy is the Lord God Almighty; the whole earth is full of his glory." Seraphim are only described fully in one place in the bible. (Isaiah). Apparently, Isaiah had a vision. (There seems to be a lot of that going on in the bible.) In Isaiah's vision the seraphim each have six wings, but they only use two of them for flying. The other wings are for covering various body parts. Two wings must cover their faces because they fly close to God and his full glory would be too powerful to behold. Two wings must cover their feet because feet are not worthy to be shown to God.

Cherubim are described in Genesis and Ezekial. They are not called angels, as they do not serve as God's messengers. In Genesis they guard the entrance to the Garden of Eden after the expulsion of Adam and Eve. See my chapter "Atrocities and Silliness" to read about Ezekial's fantastic description of the Cherubim. Their job is to guard God's holy domain from any sin or corruption. They hang around the throne of God. It's unclear why people associate "Cherubs" with cute, pudgy angelic children. The bible certainly does not – in fact Cherubim are quite frightening in their appearance as portrayed in Ezekial.

"Everything happens for a reason."
Truth: The universe is random. Bad things happen to good people all the time, and for no reason whatsoever. There is absolutely no reason for a stillborn or deformed infant, other than the fact that nature sometimes goes horribly awry.

Pope Francis recently visited informally with several children, one of whom asked him why God allows children to suffer. His reply? "That is a question for which there is no answer."

"God never gives us more than we can handle."
Truth: People commit suicide every day.

"There but for the grace of God go I."
Truth: This is a thoughtless, egotistical, and disgusting thing to say. Imagine a suffering fellow

human being who is severely handicapped. Are you saying that God brought this agony upon her while sparing you? God graced you with good health while condemning her to a lifetime of suffering. How very special you must be.

"It just wasn't his time." "It was her time." This comment seems to mean that God knows the exact date and time of every human being's death, and that that time is set in stone and is unchangeable.

Truth: People who say this do not really believe it. If they did, they wouldn't bother to schedule doctor's appointments, take medication, or undergo life-saving surgery. If you really believed this, you would allow your children to play in traffic. You could jump from a fifty story building with no fear, because if it's not "your time" you won't die.

"Everything happens for the best."

Truth: THINK before you say this. Visit a hospital where children are suffering from and dying of cancer. Remember the millions murdered during the Holocaust, The Inquisition, The Crusades. Those things did not happen for the best. Typhoons, earthquakes, floods, disease, and famine are but a few of the natural earthly perils that must be dealt with. They are not for the best.

Prayer works.
Truth: No, it doesn't.

In 2006, results of a study called The Great Prayer Experiment were published in the American Heart Journal. The theory being tested was that praying for hospital patients with serious heart conditions would improve their health. All patients had the same level of heart disease. There can be no doubt that the study was honestly conducted because it was approved by Russell Stannard who is a well known physicist and also a very religious man. The study was funded by the religiously affiliated Templeton Foundation. The patients were divided into three groups: received many prayers and didn't know it, received no prayers and didn't know it (the control group), received many prayers and did know it. Results showed no difference between those who received prayers and those who did not. A very interesting outcome was that those who received prayers and DID know it had significantly more medical complications than any other group. It was surmised that perhaps the knowledge that so many people were praying for them made the third group anxious and caused stress related illnesses. (I must be really sick if I am in the group receiving the most prayers)

Naturally, religious zealots try to rationalize, sometimes in the most reprehensible ways. A noted Oxford theologian has found a way to explain why extreme suffering occurs even though prayers are offered. The prayers of the Jews murdered in the holocaust were not answered because God wanted to give them the wonderful opportunity to show courage. At the same time, he gave the rest of us a golden opportunity to show sympathy. Japanese civilians were killed by the atomic bomb for the same reasons. I can only hope that the god he believes in will honor him by bestowing upon him the beautiful privilege of dying in agony in order to provide him opportunity for courage. The rest of us will receive the wonderful gift of sympathy. I don't know how much sympathy I could muster.

If you pray and your prayer seems to have been answered, that proves nothing but coincidence. I can get the same result by praying to my potted plant.

Religion gives life purpose. Without purpose, life is not worth living.

Truth: It is what it is. We are simply the products of evolution. Life really does not have any purpose other than what we ourselves give it. We are the only members of the animal kingdom who (unfortunately?) have awareness. We know we will die. But while we are here, we should try to have a good time. I'm by nature a happy, well adjusted person. And I, along with countless other atheists, am proof that it's possible to be such a person without concocting a way out of the human condition. Take pleasure in your life! Don't waste it by dwelling on a future that isn't real. If you must insist on a 'purpose' for your life, have it be to fully enjoy the moment.

The United States of America was founded on Christian principles by Christian men.

Diane Rogers

Truth: No, it wasn't. John Adams (our second president) as stated in his own personal letters: "This would be the best of all possible worlds if there were no religion in it."

Thomas Jefferson in a letter to John Adams dated April 11, 1823: "The day will come when the mystical generation of Jesus, by the supreme being as his father in the womb of a virgin, will be classed with the fable of the generation of Minerva in the brain of Jupiter."

The Reverend Bird Wilson, a few years removed from being a contemporary of the founding fathers, undertook the task of examining the religious beliefs of the better known of them. He scrupulously examined papers and letters and declared that he had been unable to find anything remotely resembling a belief in Christianity in their writings. He stated in one of his sermons that "the founders of our nation were nearly all infidels, and of the presidents who have thus far been elected (Washington, Adams, Jefferson, Madison, Monroe, J.Q. Adams, and Jackson)- not one professed a belief in Christianity". Wilson went on to say that during the framing of the constitution, "God was neglected. He was not merely forgotten. He was absolutely voted out of the Constitution."

There is not one mention of God in the Constitution. Some people mistakenly insist there is, but in actuality the only mention is found in the Declaration of Independence ("endowed by their creator with certain inalienable rights")

"The government of the United States of America is not, in any sense, founded on the Christian religion" (found in Article 11 of the Treaty of Tripoli)

"Fix reason in her seat, and call to her tribunal every fact, every opinion. Question with boldness even the existence of a god; because, if there be one he must approve the homage of reason rather than of blindfolded fear. Do not be frightened from this inquiry by any fear of its consequences." (In a letter from Thomas Jefferson to Peter Carr August 10, 1787. It's interesting that the word "god" was intentionally written in lower case by Mr. Jefferson.)

"When a religion is good, I conceive it will support itself, and when it does not support itself, and God does not take care to support it so that its professors are obligated to call for help of the civil power, it's a sign, I apprehend, of its being a bad one." (Benjamin Franklin October 9, 1780)

Our founders sincerely wished to establish a nation free of religious intolerance. The first amendment clearly states: "Congress shall make no law respecting an establishment of religion, or prohibiting the free exercise thereof".

While the majority of the founders were certainly not Christian, in all fairness it should be noted that many of them were Deists. Deism asserts that a creator may have created the universe, but he had no further interest in it – leaving all his creation to fend for itself. However, these men lived in a time devoid of the knowledge we now have. If they had been privy to the likes of Charles Darwin and the monumental achievements of modern day science, they would have been atheists.

But the country must have been founded upon Christianity. Why else would our coinage say "In God We Trust" and our Pledge of Allegiance contain the words "under God"? In God We Trust was added to our coins in 1956 during the McCarthy era when "godless communists" lurked around every corner. The words "under God" were added to the Pledge in 1954 for the same reason. How sad this would have made the founders.

The Immaculate Conception refers to the birth of Jesus.

Truth: The Immaculate Conception refers to the birth of the Virgin Mary.

The fact that Mary was, and remained for the entirety of her life, a virgin, is verified by the bible.

Truth: The reference to the mother of Jesus as a virgin is due to a mistranslation. The Hebrew word "almah" means 'young woman', not virgin as mistranslated from the Hebrew. Could it be that the immense amount of adoration bestowed upon Mary, in large part because of her virginal status, is undeserved? Although one might wonder why the bible and the Catholic Church are so enamored of virginity. The bible contains countless passages saying that women who are not virgins should be murdered (probably by men who are not virgins).

The very word "immaculate" insinuates that virginity is clean and sex is dirty.

We are saved by faith only.
Truth: There is only one passage in the bible that has the words faith and only together. It says: "not by faith only" and is found in James 2:2

The souls of the deceased rise to heaven or descend to hell immediately upon death.
Truth: Unknown to many Christians is the fact that this statement has been hotly debated among churchmen for centuries. The bible is not at all clear on the question of where a soul goes immediately following physical death.

"No biblical text authorizes the statement that the soul is separated from the body at the moment of death" (Interpreters Dictionary of the Bible: Vol. 1, p. 8)

"It is, indeed, very generally supposed that the souls of good men, as soon as they are discharged from the body, go directly to heaven. But this opinion has not the least foundation in the oracles of God." (John Wesley)

Modern church scholars know that the idea of souls immediately ascending to heaven upon the death of the physical body is not found in the bible. In fact, it is a pagan belief. The ascension of the soul upon death was considered heresy and was not taught as truth by the Christian church until three hundred years after the death of Christ.

Diane Rogers

Easter is a sacred Christian holiday, having its roots in the celebration of the resurrection of Christ.

Truth: Easter does in fact celebrate the resurrection of Christ for Christians. But the history and traditions of this holiday go further back than to the time of Christ. In fact, Easter is named for the pagan goddess Eastre. The female hormone estrogen is derived from her name. Eastre was a fertility goddess and her sacred animal was the rabbit, hence the origin of Easter bunnies. As for Easter eggs, eggs are the obvious symbol for fertility. Pagan mythology says that the universe was hatched from an egg.

Why is Easter celebrated on different dates each year? Christians believe that the Last Supper was a Passover Seder, since Jesus was a Jew. Therefore they wanted Easter to be celebrated around the time of the Jewish Passover. But Christians use a solar calendar and Jews use a lunar one. The dates of lunar holidays are always different. To settle things, the Council of Nicea said in 325CE that the Christian Easter would be the first Sunday after the first full moon that occurs around the Vernal Equinox (approximately March 21st). The very different cycles of the sun and the moon make it difficult for solar and lunar calendars to work together. That's why there is a movement underway among Christians to set the date of Easter as a specific day and month.

Chapter 12

I WAS JUST THINKING
SACRILEGIOUS THOUGHTS

I was just thinking about those people who
believe finding a penny means something. To be
specific, they think it means that a loved one in
heaven is trying to tell the loved one who picks it up
that they are happy and with Jesus. I wonder why
Jesus (or God) has a stockpile of pennies in heaven.
I mean, why the only coin that people routinely
throw onto the ground? Why the only coin that no
one (other than the above mentioned) will stoop to
pick up? I see pennies on the ground or the floor all
the time. If it really is a heavenly sign, why not drop
silver dollars for instance? At least drop quarters.
I might take note if I saw silver dollars at the
frequency I see pennies. I was just wondering.

I was just thinking about the way God plays Hide
and Seek with us. Why won't he show himself? He
occasionally did in Old Testament days. In Genesis

chapter 18, he even came down to earth and had a picnic with Abraham. Isn't our potato salad good too? Another Genesis story has him coming down to wrestle with Jacob. Exodus 33: 18-23 is a humorous story wherein Moses attempts to look at God. The Supreme Being tells Moses that catching a glimpse of his face will cause certain death. However, his "back parts" are not off limits. So Moses is allowed to look at God's rear end, but not his face.

I was just thinking about the notion that God is perfect. Wouldn't that mean that he would never, ever tell a lie? God promises in Deuteronomy 7:14-15 that all who follow his laws will never be childless, nor will they ever become ill. Obviously, that's not true. Read for yourself (if you can stand it) Deuteronomy 28:15-68 and discover the horrible punishments God promises if you don't believe and obey every commandment of his. I think he lied, because I'm a non-believer and I've never been subjected to pestilence, consumption, never ending fever, inflammation, extreme burning, sword thrusts, blasting, and mildew. And I don't believe my carcass will be meat unto the beasts of the earth. I've never been afflicted with emerods, scabs, and an itch that never heals. My ox has not been slain, nor my ass taken violently away.

And if God is perfect, shouldn't he be able to do anything? Judges 1:19 says that God failed to eject people from a valley because he was unable to move their iron chariots.

Why did Jesus lie about his imminent return after the crucifixion? In Matthew 16:27-28 Jesus promises those alive at that time that they will not die until his return. Read on to verse 34 where he tells them their generation will see him standing on clouds along with angels with trumpets. He tells his followers in 1 Peter 4:7 that the end is "at hand". Believers have been waiting for more than two thousand years.

A NEW AGE OF REASON?

Most recent polls I have examined agree upon the number of people declaring themselves as atheists at around 5% of the U.S. population. In a nation of 300,000,000, that means that 15,000,000 of us are atheists. I suspect the number is much higher. Politicians cannot expect election to office if they openly admit to being atheists. It's difficult to go against deeply imbedded family values. Many sensitive and good people understandably do not want to cause their family members undue pain, especially if those family members regard their faith as the cornerstone of their existence.

That being said, let's look at the percentage of declared atheists in several countries in 2005 and then again in 2012. Japan- 23% in 2005 and 31% in 2012, an increase in number of atheists of 8%; France – 14% in 2005 and 29% in 2012, an increase in number of atheists of 15%; Netherlands – 7% in 2005 and 14% in 2012, an increase in number of atheists of 7%; and finally United States – 1% in 2005 and 5% in 2012, an increase of number of atheists of 4%.

At the beginning of 2014, a Pew Research Center's Religion and Public Life Project survey revealed that only 67% of Democrats in public life declared a belief in evolution. As if that fact is not embarrassing enough, only 43% of Republicans do. As late as 2014, more Republicans believe that "humans and all other living things have existed in their present form since the beginning of time" than believe in evolution. The percentage of all adults polled showed 60% believe in evolution. 78% of mainline Protestants and 68% of white Catholics believe in evolution. Among Hispanic Catholics and black Protestants, the percentage is lower. (only 53% Hispanics and 44% black). White evangelical Protestants have the dubious honor of having the greatest number of evolution-deniers in their midst. Only 27% of them believe in evolution.

A 2012 Gallop International poll asked 51,927 people world-wide the following question: "Would you say you are a religious person, not a religious person, or a convinced atheist?" 59% declared themselves religious, 23% not religious, and 13% convinced atheists. 5% did not know. In the United States, 60% said they were religious (it was 73% in 2005), 30% said they were not religious, 5% identified as convinced atheists (it was 1% in 2005). 5% did not know.

Conclusion

As mentioned before, the bible is undergoing many changes. Not only are changes being made to make the bible more gender-friendly, the more obscene and ridiculous passages are being omitted in works such as "Chord" in order to slow the retreat of congregants. If you are a church goer, you already know that in mainstream churches the pastor or priest neglects to quote from those passages. It's always the uplifting and non controversial passages that are included in the sermon. Do you attend bible study? Are any of the passages mentioned in chapter two ever discussed in any meaningful way, or are they quickly dismissed? Or in more likelihood, not discussed at all?

In many churches in America today, the stilted language of the bible has been replaced with modern English. No more thees and thous. A phrase such as "whither thou goest" is replaced with "wherever you go".

Recently it's been hinted that the Catholic Church is reconsidering its policy as regards marriage and the priesthood. Why is it that church leaders have never been allowed to marry? How amusing that apologists suggest the policy originated to ensure that men would be able to devote all their energies to the service of the Lord, without the distraction of wife and family. Read again the descriptions of the hatred directed against women by both the authors of the bible and early churchmen. The holiest of holy men (often made saints) were those who distanced themselves from women. It was unthinkable that church leaders would allow themselves to associate with and be contaminated by women. If you have any doubt, you have only to look closely at the infrastructure of the Vatican- a gathering of celibate old men who delight in adorning themselves with finery and giving one another titles such as Father, Eminence, Your Grace, and Holiness.

In this book, all bible references are from the King James Version which my grandmother gave me in 1950. The fly leaf says, "translated out of the original tongues and with the former translations diligently compared and revised". So even in 1950 the bible was revised.

Revelation says says that no man may take anything away from the original text. If he does, he will be removed from God's book of life. Jesus Christ says in Matthew 5:17-18 that not one "jot or tittle" may be changed in the bible, which is law.

Yes, there are passages in the bible which are uplifting and beautiful. But does that overshadow the obscene and ridiculous ones? One cannot conveniently sweep some things under the rug and focus only on that which one agrees with. Either the bible contains the absolute word of God and ALL things written in it are sanctioned by him, or it is a work of fiction. Picking and choosing is not an option.

Why are people so willing to believe the unbelievable? I found this wonderful quote on the internet and sadly could not find the author's name. It sums up so perfectly the reason for much religious belief: "I am a geologist, for the Earth, she calls to me. I am an astronomer, for the Cosmos, she calls to me. I am a biologist, for Life, she calls to me. I am a physicist, for Nature, she calls to me. I am a young earth creationist, for that other stuff frightens and confuses me."

"When I look up at the starry heavens at night, it is not the works of some god that I see there. I am face to face with a power that baffles speech. I see no lineaments of personality. The universe is so unhuman. It goes its own way with so little thought of man. We must adjust our notions to the discovery that things are not shaped to us, but that we are shaped to them. The air was not made for our lungs, but we have lungs because there is air. The light was not created for our eyes, but we have eyes because there is light. All the forces of nature are going their own way. Man avails himself of them, or catches a ride as best he can. We must and will get used to the chill.... the cosmic chill. Every day is a Sabbath to me. All pure water is holy water, and this earth is a celestial abode." (John Burroughs)

AMEN